MAPS
of the
World

A Reproducible Workbook
and Curriculum Guide

Emerald
Books

P.O. BOX 635, LYNNWOOD, WA 98046

Emerald Books are distributed through YWAM Publishing. For a full list of titles, visit our website at www.ywampublishing.com or call 1-800-922-2143.

Maps of the World: A Reproducible Workbook and Curriculum Guide
Copyright © 2007 by The Emerald Book Company

12 11 10 09 08 07   10 9 8 7 6 5 4 3 2 1

Published by Emerald Books
P.O. Box 635
Lynnwood, Washington 98046

ISBN-10: 1-932096-46-9
ISBN-13: 978-1-932096-46-0

Printed in the United States of America.

Contents

Introduction

Designed for use in schools and homeschools, *Maps of the World* is a reproducible resource suitable for students of a variety of ages, abilities, and learning styles. The student worksheets and maps may be duplicated for use by more than one student.* Or one student can write directly in the workbook, so that in the end he or she has a bound reference book and keepsake of his or her mapping work and fact sheets.

At the prompting of teachers* who use our *Maps of the United States* workbook and other resources in their school and homeschool curriculum, we at Emerald Books have prepared this second collection of hand-drawn maps, worksheets, and activities to further support the study of geography, this time on a global scale.

Reproducible maps and worksheets. At the heart of *Maps of the World* are the reproducible maps and worksheets for the world's continents and countries. Included with these are two world maps and worksheets as well as maps and worksheets for Antarctica and the Arctic.

The maps and worksheets are arranged by continent. Each continental section begins with both a political and physical map of the continent, along with worksheets designed to give students an overview of the continent and guide them in mapping its nations, capitals, and major geographical features. Following each continent overview are larger-scale regional maps showing several countries, or more rarely, because of its size or location, a single country. Each regional or country map is faced by a Map It! worksheet that aids students in mapping important cities and geographical features. This is followed by fact worksheets for each country that appears on the map.

The stylized, hand-drawn maps featured in *Maps of the World* are intended to encourage creativity and craftsmanship in the student's own work. Mountains, rivers, and lakes are indicated, but not labeled, on the maps. At the edges of the maps, stippling distinguishes land borders from surrounding waters. Each regional and country map page includes a compass and scale as well as a small locator map so that students can easily identify the region or country's location. If students complete the relevant political and physical continent maps first, they can also refer to their own maps for context.

The *Maps of the World* worksheets are designed to initiate a student's research. Fact worksheets that cover parallel entities (e.g., countries or continents) are largely identical so that students gather parallel information about them. This will enable students to make comparisons as they learn about such factors as geographic extremes, population and area, type of government, major religions and languages, and economic well-being. In the same way, mapping worksheets that cover parallel entities are largely identical, prompting students to recognize that some areas are rich in one geographical feature while others are dominated by a different feature. Because the worksheets are identical in most respects, students should be alerted that not every region or country has every feature listed on the worksheets or in the mapping directions. As students gather their data and discover that a feature is missing, they will have learned something about the region or country.

In addition to the maps and worksheets, *Maps of the World* contains many other helps for studying geography.

Additional mapping activities. A resource for the teacher, Appendix A contains additional mapping activities that help students explore the world through thematic mapping. We suggest that you photocopy the world maps and the maps of the continents before they are used so that they can be duplicated for additional mapping activities, such as those suggested in this appendix.

Student explorations. Appendix B contains many diverse activities from which you can choose, providing students of different ages, abilities, and learning styles with a forum to delve deeper into learning about the countries of the world. Suggested activities include report writing, creative writing, oral presentations, and hands-on activities like three-dimensional map modeling and creating timelines, brochures, and children's books. The activities require a varying amount of research and can be made more or less comprehensive at your discretion. Choose the activities that are best suited to your student or students.

Conceptual social studies exercises. The conceptual social studies exercises in Appendix C involve brief activities like comparing areas and populations and studying maps of population density. Students can engage in these exercises through group discussions, paragraph writing, or short oral reports.

Vocabulary. Appendix D provides a list of terms related to geography and cartography, ranging from the simple to the complex, and gives ideas for studying them.

Resources. Appendix E describes some of the many good resources available for studying geography and cartography. The featured resources include books, Internet sites, and subscription sites available free of charge through many libraries and schools.

Student instructions. In addition to the flexibility of choosing which activities to do, which countries to cover, and what order to follow, this workbook gives you the freedom to provide specific instructions for the worksheet and mapping activities, recognizing that this will depend on a student's grade level and learning goals.

Depending on their learning objectives, students may benefit from specific guidelines for using color, how to indicate the different features (such as river basins and deserts) and how to label the various classes of items (such as rivers, countries, capital cities, and other cities). Students of all ages may need a reminder to be aware of the locations of all items they are mapping before they actually begin so that they can use the space well and create a clean, attractive map. Younger students especially may want to write their labels in light pencil first.

To supplement the favorite resources you may already use, Appendix E refers you to many good sources of the information required for the worksheets and mapping activities. Students may also enjoy studying examples of published maps, both historical and contemporary, to become familiar with mapping conventions and styles.

One of our goals at Emerald Books has been to encourage a global outlook and an appreciation for the nations and peoples of the world. In keeping with this vision, *Maps of the World* provides another creative vehicle for learning about the world and its peoples, this time through the fascinating study of geography. We hope that you and your students enjoy the journey.

---

*For the sake of brevity in the instructions, the word *teacher* includes the homeschooling parent and the word *student* refers to a child either in a traditional classroom or in a homeschool environment.

The World

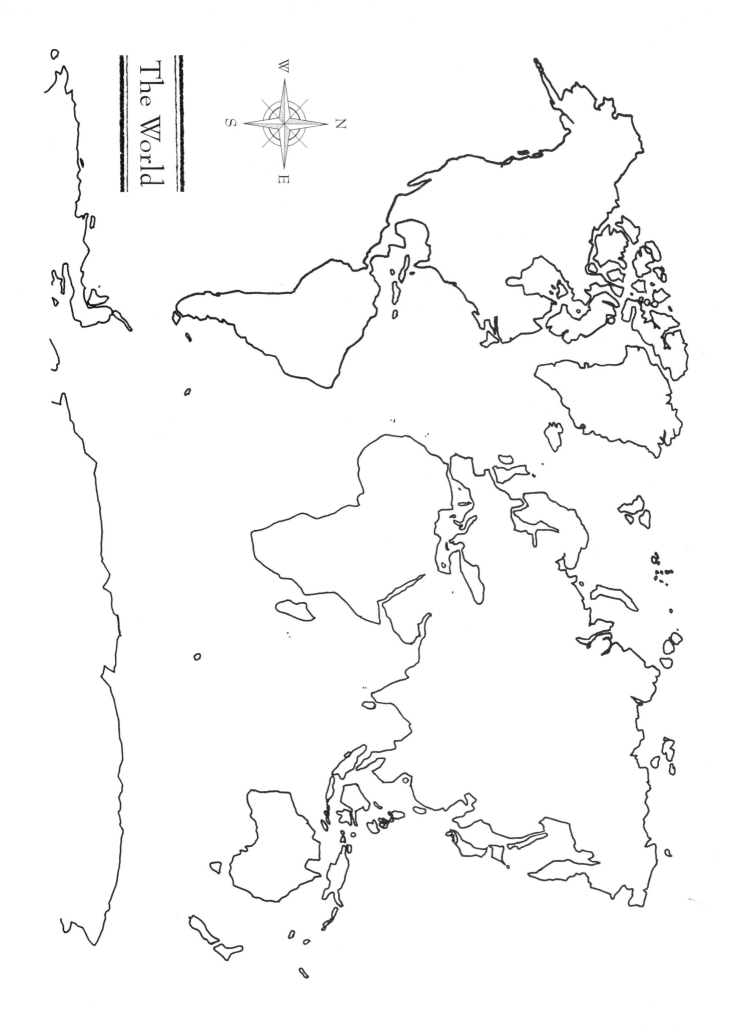

The World

The World

Gather these facts about the earth's physical geography, filling in the blanks.

Total area _____ Land area _____ Water area _____

Percentage of the world's surface that is water _____

Distance around the Equator _____

The seven continents (largest to smallest) _____

_____

The five oceans (largest to smallest) _____

_____

Highest point and its elevation _____

Lowest point and its elevation _____

Longest river _____

Second and third longest rivers _____

Largest freshwater lake _____

Largest saltwater lake _____

Largest sea _____

Largest hot desert _____

Largest cold desert _____

Largest island _____

Wettest place _____

Driest place _____

Hottest place _____

Coldest place _____

Map It!

On the world outline map, label the world's continents and oceans and the geographic extremes from the worksheet above. Before labeling the continents, sketch in the three longest rivers and consider the locations of the geographic extremes so that you can use the space well. Finally, using colored pencils, mark the boundaries of the continents, and shade each continent a different color.

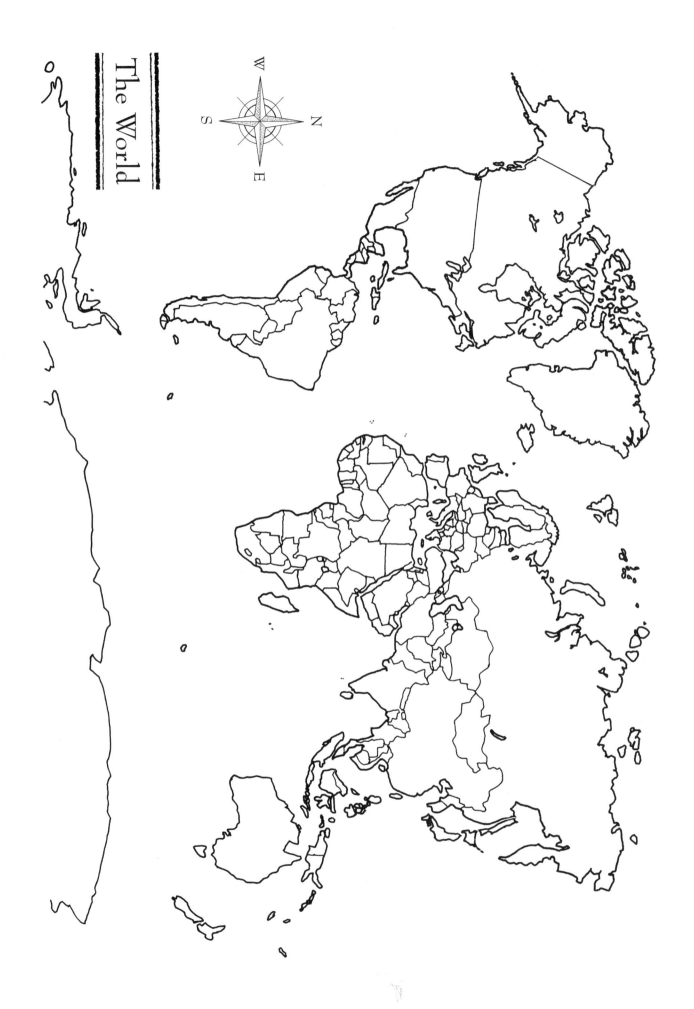

The World

The World

Gather these facts about the world and its people, filling in the blanks.

Current population _____

Life expectancy _____ men _____ women   Literacy _____ % male _____ % female

Major religions _____

_____

Major languages _____

_____

Number of independent countries _____

Largest country _____

Smallest country _____

Most populous country _____

Least populous country _____

Most densely populated country _____

Least densely populated country _____

Newest country _____

Longest border _____

Five largest cities and their populations _____

_____

Five largest metropolitan areas and their populations _____

_____

Most northerly inhabited place _____

Most southerly inhabited place _____

Map It!

On the world political map, label the geographic extremes from the worksheet above. Before beginning, create a key for your map using colors and symbols. For example, which color indicates the largest country and which the smallest? Which symbol marks the largest cities and which the most northerly and southerly inhabited places?

North America

North America

North America

Gather these facts about the continent of North America, filling in the blanks.

Total land area _____ Rank in area _____ of 7

Total population _____ Rank in population _____ of 7

Major languages _____

Major religions _____

Major natural resources _____

Longest river _____

Highest mountain _____

Lowest point _____

Largest lake _____

Biggest desert _____

Biggest island _____

Three largest cities _____

Number of independent countries _____

Largest country _____

Smallest country _____

Most populous country _____

Least populous country _____

Most densely populated country _____

Least densely populated country _____

Largest dependent territory _____

Smallest dependent territory _____

Most populous dependent territory _____

Map It!

On the political map of North America, label each independent country and its capital. Then use colored pencils to make each country a different color than the countries that border it.

North America

Map It!

Use this worksheet to organize your information as you research the following geographical features of North America. This will help you be aware of the locations of all the items you will map before you actually begin so that you can use the space well. Finally, mark each item on the physical map of the continent.

North America's major landforms (e.g., mountain ranges, plains, plateaus) _____
_____
_____
_____

North America's major rivers and river basins _____
_____
_____
_____

North America's major inland bodies of water _____
_____
_____

North America's deserts _____
_____
_____

North America's major islands, peninsulas, and capes _____
_____
_____

Bodies of water that border North America _____
_____
_____

North America's highest and lowest points and their elevations _____
_____

Any of the following lines of latitude that intersect North America: Arctic Circle, Tropic of Cancer, Equator, Tropic of Capricorn, Antarctic Circle _____
_____
_____

Any other special geographical features _____
_____
_____

Canada

0 100 200 300

Miles

N W E S

Map It!

Use this worksheet to organize your information as you research the following geographical features of Canada. This will help you be aware of the locations of all the items you will map before you actually begin so that you can use the space well. If Canada doesn't have one of the features listed, simply write "none" on the blank line. Finally, mark each item on the map of the country.

Canada's capital city _____

Canada's five largest cities _____

_____

Canada's major landforms (e.g., mountain ranges, plains, plateaus) _____

_____

_____

_____

Canada's highest and lowest points and their elevations _____

_____

Canada's major rivers and river basins _____

_____

_____

_____

Canada's major inland bodies of water _____

_____

_____

Canada's deserts _____

_____

Canada's important islands, peninsulas, and capes _____

_____

_____

Bodies of water that border Canada _____

_____

_____

Any other special geographical features _____

_____

Canada

Gather these facts about Canada, filling in the blanks.

Capital _____ Type of government _____

Date of independence _____ From _____

Chief of state _____

Head of government _____

Name for citizen (e.g., Australian) _____

Current population _____ World rank in population _____

Life expectancy _____ men _____ women Literacy _____ % male _____ % female

Ethnic groups _____

Major religions _____

Major languages _____

Land area _____ Water area _____ World rank in area _____

Five largest cities and their populations _____

_____

Bordering nations _____

_____

Climate _____

Terrain _____

Highest point and its elevation _____

Lowest point and its elevation _____

GDP _____ Per capita GDP _____ World rank in GDP _____

Major natural resources _____

Major industries _____

Chief agricultural products _____

Major exports _____

Major imports _____

United States of America

0
150
300
Miles

0
30
60
Miles

0 50 100   200   400
Miles

W

S   N

E

Map It!

Use this worksheet to organize your information as you research the following geographical features of the United States of America. This will help you be aware of the locations of all the items you will map before you actually begin so that you can use the space well. If the United States doesn't have one of the features listed, simply write "none" on the blank line. Finally, mark each item on the map of the country.

The capital city of the United States _____

The five largest cities in the United States _____

_____

The major landforms of the United States (e.g., mountain ranges, plains, plateaus) _____

_____

_____

_____

The highest and lowest points in the United States and their elevations _____

_____

The major rivers and river basins of the United States _____

_____

_____

_____

The major inland bodies of water of the United States _____

_____

_____

The deserts of the United States _____

_____

The important islands, peninsulas, and capes of the United States _____

_____

_____

Bodies of water that border the United States _____

_____

_____

Any other special geographical features _____

_____

United States of America

Gather these facts about the United States of America, filling in the blanks.

Capital _____ Type of government _____

Date of independence _____ From _____

Chief of state _____

Head of government _____

Name for citizen (e.g., Canadian) _____

Current population _____ World rank in population _____

Life expectancy _____ men _____ women Literacy _____ % male _____ % female

Ethnic groups _____

Major religions _____

Major languages _____

Land area _____ Water area _____ World rank in area _____

Five largest cities and their populations _____

_____

Bordering nations _____

_____

Climate _____

Terrain _____

Highest point and its elevation _____

Lowest point and its elevation _____

GDP _____ Per capita GDP _____ World rank in GDP _____

Major natural resources _____

Major industries _____

Chief agricultural products _____

Major exports _____

Major imports _____

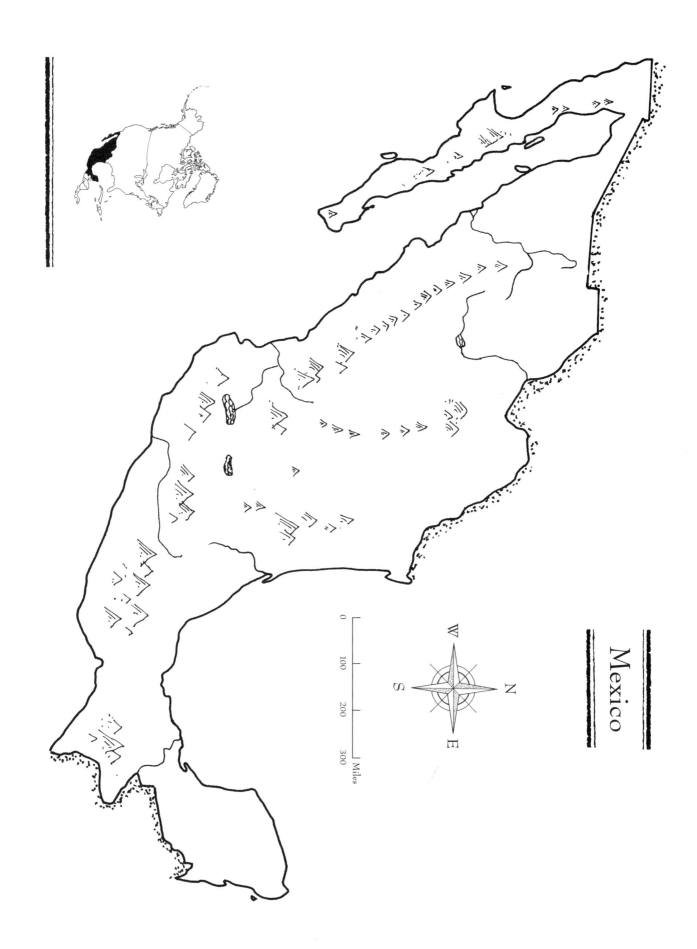

Mexico

Map It!

Use this worksheet to organize your information as you research the following geographical features of Mexico. This will help you be aware of the locations of all the items you will map before you actually begin so that you can use the space well. If Mexico doesn't have one of the features listed, simply write "none" on the blank line. Finally, mark each item on the map of the country.

Mexico's capital city _____

Mexico's five largest cities _____

_____

Mexico's major landforms (e.g., mountain ranges, plains, plateaus) _____

_____

_____

_____

Mexico's highest and lowest points and their elevations _____

_____

Mexico's major rivers and river basins _____

_____

_____

_____

Mexico's major inland bodies of water _____

_____

_____

Mexico's deserts _____

_____

Mexico's important islands, peninsulas, and capes _____

_____

_____

Bodies of water that border Mexico _____

_____

_____

Any other special geographical features _____

_____

Mexico

Gather these facts about Mexico, filling in the blanks.

Capital _____ Type of government _____

Date of independence _____ From _____

Chief of state _____

Head of government _____

Name for citizen (e.g., Canadian) _____

Current population _____ World rank in population _____

Life expectancy _____ men _____ women Literacy _____ % male _____ % female

Ethnic groups _____

Major religions _____

Major languages _____

Land area _____ Water area _____ World rank in area _____

Five largest cities and their populations _____

_____

Bordering nations _____

_____

Climate _____

Terrain _____

Highest point and its elevation _____

Lowest point and its elevation _____

GDP _____ Per capita GDP _____ World rank in GDP _____

Major natural resources _____

Major industries _____

Chief agricultural products _____

Major exports _____

Major imports _____

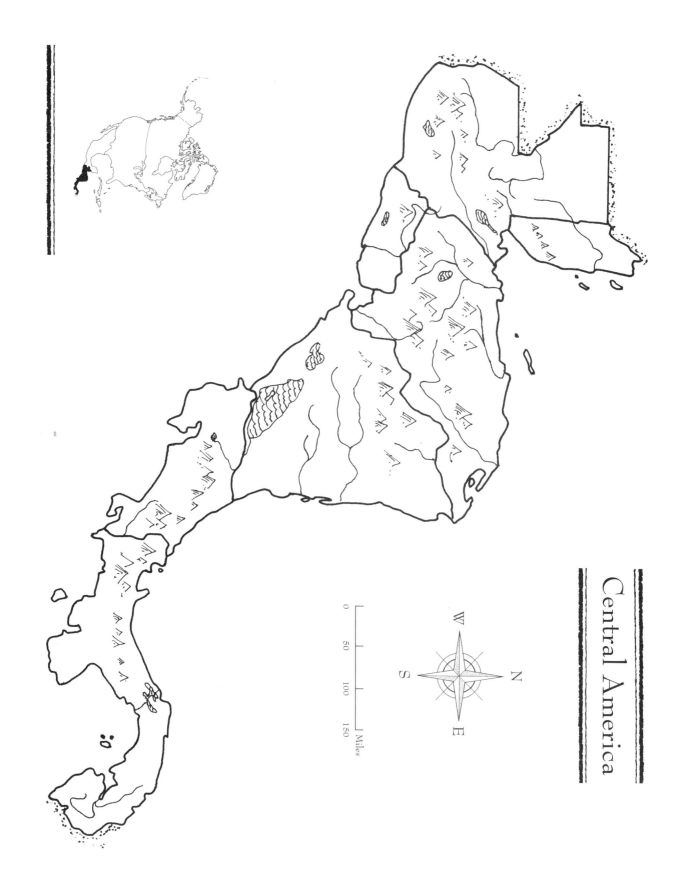

Central America

W N E S

0 50 100 150 Miles

Map It!

Use this worksheet to organize your information as you research the following geographical features of Central America. This will help you be aware of the locations of all the items you will map before you actually begin so that you can use the space well. If the region doesn't have one of the features listed, simply write "none" on the blank line. Finally, mark each item on the map of the region.

The name of each independent country and its capital city _____

_____

_____

_____

Five other important cities in the region _____

_____

The region's major landforms (e.g., mountain ranges, plains, plateaus) _____

_____

_____

_____

The region's major rivers and river basins _____

_____

_____

_____

The region's major inland bodies of water _____

_____

_____

The region's deserts _____

_____

The region's important islands, peninsulas, and capes _____

_____

_____

Bodies of water that border the region _____

_____

_____

Any other special geographical features _____

_____

Belize

Gather these facts about Belize, filling in the blanks.

Capital _____ Type of government _____

Date of independence _____ From _____

Chief of state _____

Head of government _____

Name for citizen (e.g., Canadian) _____

Current population _____ World rank in population _____

Life expectancy _____ men _____ women Literacy _____ % male _____ % female

Ethnic groups _____

Major religions _____

Major languages _____

Land area _____ Water area _____ World rank in area _____

Five largest cities and their populations _____

_____

Bordering nations _____

_____

Climate _____

Terrain _____

Highest point and its elevation _____

Lowest point and its elevation _____

GDP _____ Per capita GDP _____ World rank in GDP _____

Major natural resources _____

Major industries _____

Chief agricultural products _____

Major exports _____

Major imports _____

Costa Rica

Gather these facts about Costa Rica, filling in the blanks.

Capital _____ Type of government _____

Date of independence _____ From _____

Chief of state _____

Head of government _____

Name for citizen (e.g., Canadian) _____

Current population _____ World rank in population _____

Life expectancy _____ men _____ women Literacy _____ % male _____ % female

Ethnic groups _____

Major religions _____

Major languages _____

Land area _____ Water area _____ World rank in area _____

Five largest cities and their populations _____

_____

Bordering nations _____

_____

Climate _____

Terrain _____

Highest point and its elevation _____

Lowest point and its elevation _____

GDP _____ Per capita GDP _____ World rank in GDP _____

Major natural resources _____

Major industries _____

Chief agricultural products _____

Major exports _____

Major imports _____

El Salvador

Gather these facts about El Salvador, filling in the blanks.

Capital _____ Type of government _____

Date of independence _____ From _____

Chief of state _____

Head of government _____

Name for citizen (e.g., Canadian) _____

Current population _____ World rank in population _____

Life expectancy _____ men _____ women Literacy _____ % male _____ % female

Ethnic groups _____

Major religions _____

Major languages _____

Land area _____ Water area _____ World rank in area _____

Five largest cities and their populations _____

_____

Bordering nations _____

_____

Climate _____

Terrain _____

Highest point and its elevation _____

Lowest point and its elevation _____

GDP _____ Per capita GDP _____ World rank in GDP _____

Major natural resources _____

Major industries _____

Chief agricultural products _____

Major exports _____

Major imports _____

Guatemala

Gather these facts about Guatemala, filling in the blanks.

Capital _____ Type of government _____

Date of independence _____ From _____

Chief of state _____

Head of government _____

Name for citizen (e.g., Canadian) _____

Current population _____ World rank in population _____

Life expectancy _____ men _____ women   Literacy _____ % male _____ % female

Ethnic groups _____

Major religions _____

Major languages _____

Land area _____ Water area _____ World rank in area _____

Five largest cities and their populations _____

_____

Bordering nations _____

_____

Climate _____

Terrain _____

Highest point and its elevation _____

Lowest point and its elevation _____

GDP _____ Per capita GDP _____ World rank in GDP _____

Major natural resources _____

Major industries _____

Chief agricultural products _____

Major exports _____

Major imports _____

Honduras

Gather these facts about Honduras, filling in the blanks.

Capital _____ Type of government _____

Date of independence _____ From _____

Chief of state _____

Head of government _____

Name for citizen (e.g., Canadian) _____

Current population _____ World rank in population _____

Life expectancy _____ men _____ women   Literacy _____ % male _____ % female

Ethnic groups _____

Major religions _____

Major languages _____

Land area _____ Water area _____ World rank in area _____

Five largest cities and their populations _____

_____

Bordering nations _____

_____

Climate _____

Terrain _____

Highest point and its elevation _____

Lowest point and its elevation _____

GDP _____ Per capita GDP _____ World rank in GDP _____

Major natural resources _____

Major industries _____

Chief agricultural products _____

Major exports _____

Major imports _____

Nicaragua

Gather these facts about Nicaragua, filling in the blanks.

Capital _____ Type of government _____

Date of independence _____ ____ From _____

Chief of state _____

Head of government _____

Name for citizen (e.g., Canadian) _____

Current population _____ World rank in population _____

Life expectancy _____ men _____ women   Literacy _____ % male _____ % female

Ethnic groups _____

Major religions _____

Major languages _____

Land area _____ Water area _____ World rank in area _____

Five largest cities and their populations _____

_____

Bordering nations _____

_____

Climate _____

Terrain _____

Highest point and its elevation _____

Lowest point and its elevation _____

GDP_____ Per capita GDP _____ World rank in GDP _____

Major natural resources _____

Major industries _____

Chief agricultural products _____

Major exports _____

Major imports _____

Panama

Gather these facts about Panama, filling in the blanks.

Capital _____ Type of government _____

Date of independence _____ From _____

Chief of state _____

Head of government _____

Name for citizen (e.g., Canadian) _____

Current population _____ World rank in population _____

Life expectancy _____ men _____ women Literacy _____ % male _____ % female

Ethnic groups _____

Major religions _____

Major languages _____

Land area _____ Water area _____ World rank in area _____

Five largest cities and their populations _____

_____

Bordering nations _____

_____

Climate _____

Terrain _____

Highest point and its elevation _____

Lowest point and its elevation _____

GDP _____ Per capita GDP _____ World rank in GDP _____

Major natural resources _____

Major industries _____

Chief agricultural products _____

Major exports _____

Major imports _____

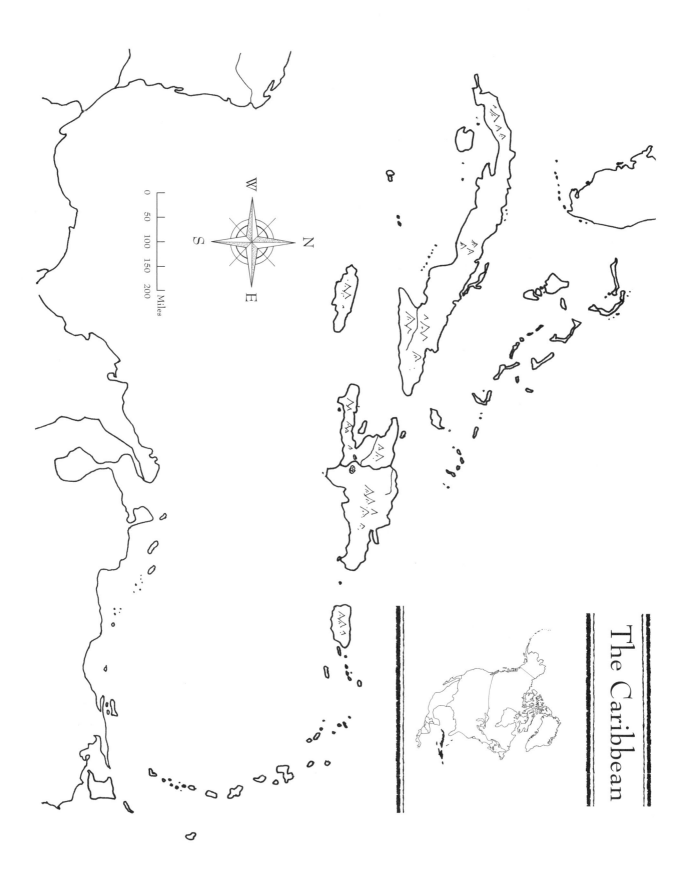

The Caribbean

Map It!

Use this worksheet to organize your information as you research the following geographical features of the Caribbean. This will help you be aware of the locations of all the items you will map before you actually begin so that you can use the space well. If the region doesn't have one of the features listed, simply write "none" on the blank line. Finally, mark each item on the map of the region.

The name of each independent country and its capital city _____

_____

_____

_____

_____

_____

_____

The region's major landforms (e.g., mountain ranges, plains, plateaus) _____

_____

_____

_____

The region's major rivers and river basins _____

_____

_____

_____

The region's major inland bodies of water _____

_____

_____

The region's deserts _____

_____

The region's important islands, peninsulas, and capes _____

_____

_____

Bodies of water that border the region _____

_____

_____

Any other special geographical features _____

_____

Antigua and Barbuda

Gather these facts about Antigua and Barbuda, filling in the blanks.

Capital _____ Type of government _____

Date of independence _____ From _____

Chief of state _____

Head of government _____

Name for citizen (e.g., Canadian) _____

Current population _____ World rank in population _____

Life expectancy _____ men _____ women   Literacy _____ % male _____ % female

Ethnic groups _____

Major religions _____

Major languages _____

Land area _____ Water area _____ World rank in area _____

Five largest cities and their populations _____

_____

Bordering nations _____

_____

Climate _____

Terrain _____

Highest point and its elevation _____

Lowest point and its elevation _____

GDP _____ Per capita GDP _____ World rank in GDP _____

Major natural resources _____

Major industries _____

Chief agricultural products _____

Major exports _____

Major imports _____

The Bahamas

Gather these facts about The Bahamas, filling in the blanks.

Capital _____ Type of government _____

Date of independence _____ From _____

Chief of state _____

Head of government _____

Name for citizen (e.g., Canadian) _____

Current population _____ World rank in population _____

Life expectancy _____ men _____ women   Literacy _____ % male _____ % female

Ethnic groups _____

Major religions _____

Major languages _____

Land area _____ Water area _____ World rank in area _____

Five largest cities and their populations _____

_____

Bordering nations _____

_____

Climate _____

Terrain _____

Highest point and its elevation _____

Lowest point and its elevation _____

GDP _____ Per capita GDP _____ World rank in GDP _____

Major natural resources _____

Major industries _____

Chief agricultural products _____

Major exports _____

Major imports _____

Barbados

Gather these facts about Barbados, filling in the blanks.

Capital _____ Type of government _____

Date of independence _____ From _____

Chief of state _____

Head of government _____

Name for citizen (e.g., Canadian) _____

Current population _____ World rank in population _____

Life expectancy _____ men _____ women   Literacy _____ % male _____ % female

Ethnic groups _____

Major religions _____

Major languages _____

Land area _____ Water area _____ World rank in area _____

Five largest cities and their populations _____

_____

Bordering nations _____

_____

Climate _____

Terrain _____

Highest point and its elevation _____

Lowest point and its elevation _____

GDP _____ Per capita GDP _____ World rank in GDP _____

Major natural resources _____

Major industries _____

Chief agricultural products _____

Major exports _____

Major imports _____

Cuba

Gather these facts about Cuba, filling in the blanks.

Capital _____ Type of government _____

Date of independence _____ From _____

Chief of state _____ _____

Head of government _____

Name for citizen (e.g., Canadian) _____

Current population _____ World rank in population _____

Life expectancy _____ men _____ women Literacy _____ % male _____ % female

Ethnic groups _____

Major religions _____

Major languages _____

Land area _____ Water area _____ World rank in area _____

Five largest cities and their populations _____

_____

Bordering nations _____

_____

Climate _____

Terrain _____

Highest point and its elevation _____

Lowest point and its elevation _____

GDP _____ Per capita GDP _____ World rank in GDP _____

Major natural resources _____

Major industries _____

Chief agricultural products _____

Major exports _____

Major imports _____

Dominica

Gather these facts about Dominica, filling in the blanks.

Capital _____ Type of government _____

Date of independence _____ From _____

Chief of state _____

Head of government _____

Name for citizen (e.g., Canadian) _____

Current population _____ World rank in population _____

Life expectancy _____ men _____ women Literacy _____ % male _____ % female

Ethnic groups _____

Major religions _____

Major languages _____

Land area _____ Water area _____ World rank in area _____

Five largest cities and their populations _____

_____

Bordering nations _____

_____

Climate _____

Terrain _____

Highest point and its elevation _____

Lowest point and its elevation _____

GDP _____ Per capita GDP _____ World rank in GDP _____

Major natural resources _____

Major industries _____

Chief agricultural products _____

Major exports _____

Major imports _____

48

Dominican Republic

Gather these facts about the Dominican Republic, filling in the blanks.

Capital _____ Type of government _____

Date of independence _____ From _____

Chief of state _____

Head of government _____

Name for citizen (e.g., Canadian) _____

Current population _____ World rank in population _____

Life expectancy _____ men _____ women Literacy _____ % male _____ % female

Ethnic groups _____

Major religions _____

Major languages _____

Land area _____ Water area _____ World rank in area _____

Five largest cities and their populations _____

_____

Bordering nations _____

_____

Climate _____

Terrain _____

Highest point and its elevation _____

Lowest point and its elevation _____

GDP _____ Per capita GDP _____ World rank in GDP _____

Major natural resources _____

Major industries _____

Chief agricultural products _____

Major exports _____

Major imports _____

Grenada

Gather these facts about Grenada, filling in the blanks.

Capital _____ Type of government _____

Date of independence _____ From _____

Chief of state _____

Head of government _____

Name for citizen (e.g., Canadian) _____

Current population _____ World rank in population _____

Life expectancy _____ men _____ women Literacy _____ % male _____ % female

Ethnic groups _____

Major religions _____

Major languages _____

Land area _____ Water area _____ World rank in area _____

Five largest cities and their populations _____

_____

Bordering nations _____

_____

Climate _____

Terrain _____

Highest point and its elevation _____

Lowest point and its elevation _____

GDP _____ Per capita GDP _____ World rank in GDP _____

Major natural resources _____

Major industries _____

Chief agricultural products _____

Major exports _____

Major imports _____

Haiti

Gather these facts about Haiti, filling in the blanks.

Capital _____ Type of government _____

Date of independence _____ From _____

Chief of state _____

Head of government _____

Name for citizen (e.g., Canadian) _____

Current population _____ World rank in population _____

Life expectancy _____ men _____ women   Literacy _____ % male _____ % female

Ethnic groups _____

Major religions _____

Major languages _____

Land area _____ Water area _____ World rank in area _____

Five largest cities and their populations _____

_____

Bordering nations _____

_____

Climate _____

Terrain _____

Highest point and its elevation _____

Lowest point and its elevation _____

GDP _____ Per capita GDP _____ World rank in GDP _____

Major natural resources _____

Major industries _____

Chief agricultural products _____

Major exports _____

Major imports _____

Jamaica

Gather these facts about Jamaica, filling in the blanks.

Capital _____ Type of government _____

Date of independence _____ From _____

Chief of state _____

Head of government _____

Name for citizen (e.g., Canadian) _____

Current population _____ World rank in population _____

Life expectancy _____ men _____ women Literacy _____ % male _____ % female

Ethnic groups _____

Major religions _____

Major languages _____

Land area _____ Water area _____ World rank in area _____

Five largest cities and their populations _____

_____

Bordering nations _____

_____

Climate _____

Terrain _____

Highest point and its elevation _____

Lowest point and its elevation _____

GDP _____ Per capita GDP _____ World rank in GDP _____

Major natural resources _____

Major industries _____

Chief agricultural products _____

Major exports _____

Major imports _____

St. Kitts and Nevis

Gather these facts about St. Kitts and Nevis, filling in the blanks.

Capital _____ Type of government _____

Date of independence _____ From _____

Chief of state _____

Head of government _____

Name for citizen (e.g., Canadian) _____

Current population _____ World rank in population _____

Life expectancy _____ men _____ women   Literacy _____ % male _____ % female

Ethnic groups _____

Major religions _____

Major languages _____

Land area _____ Water area _____ World rank in area _____

Five largest cities and their populations _____

_____

Bordering nations _____

_____

Climate _____

Terrain _____

Highest point and its elevation _____

Lowest point and its elevation _____

GDP _____ Per capita GDP _____ World rank in GDP _____

Major natural resources _____

Major industries _____

Chief agricultural products _____

Major exports _____

Major imports _____

Saint Lucia

Gather these facts about Saint Lucia, filling in the blanks.

Capital _____ Type of government _____

Date of independence _____ From _____

Chief of state _____

Head of government _____

Name for citizen (e.g., Canadian) _____

Current population _____ World rank in population _____

Life expectancy _____ men _____ women Literacy _____ % male _____ % female

Ethnic groups _____

Major religions _____

Major languages _____

Land area _____ Water area _____ World rank in area _____

Five largest cities and their populations _____

_____

Bordering nations _____

_____

Climate _____

Terrain _____

Highest point and its elevation _____

Lowest point and its elevation _____

GDP _____ Per capita GDP _____ World rank in GDP _____

Major natural resources _____

Major industries _____

Chief agricultural products _____

Major exports _____

Major imports _____

Saint Vincent and the Grenadines

Gather these facts about Saint Vincent and the Grenadines, filling in the blanks.

Capital _____ Type of government _____

Date of independence _____ From _____

Chief of state ___ _____

Head of government _____

Name for citizen (e.g., Canadian) _____

Current population _____ World rank in population _____

Life expectancy _____ men _____ women Literacy _____ % male _____ % female

Ethnic groups _____

Major religions _____

Major languages _____

Land area _____ Water area _____ World rank in area _____

Five largest cities and their populations _____

_____

Bordering nations _____

_____

Climate _____

Terrain _____

Highest point and its elevation _____

Lowest point and its elevation _____

GDP_____ Per capita GDP _____ World rank in GDP _____

Major natural resources _____

Major industries _____

Chief agricultural products _____

Major exports _____

Major imports _____

Trinidad and Tobago

Gather these facts about Trinidad and Tobago, filling in the blanks.

Capital _____ _____ Type of government _____

Date of independence _____ From _____

Chief of state _____

Head of government _____

Name for citizen (e.g., Canadian) _____

Current population _____ World rank in population _____

Life expectancy _____ men _____ women Literacy _____ % male _____ % female

Ethnic groups _____

Major religions _____

Major languages _____

Land area _____ Water area _____ World rank in area _____

Five largest cities and their populations _____

_____

Bordering nations _____

_____

Climate _____

Terrain _____

Highest point and its elevation _____

Lowest point and its elevation _____

GDP_____ Per capita GDP _____ World rank in GDP _____

Major natural resources _____

Major industries _____

Chief agricultural products _____

Major exports _____

Major imports _____

South America

South America

South America

Gather these facts about the continent of South America, filling in the blanks.

Total land area _____ Rank in area _____ of 7

Total population _____ Rank in population _____ of 7

Major languages _____

Major religions _____

Major natural resources _____

Longest river _____

Highest mountain _____

Lowest point _____

Largest lake _____

Biggest desert _____

Biggest island _____

Three largest cities _____

Number of independent countries _____

Largest country _____

Smallest country _____

Most populous country _____

Least populous country _____

Most densely populated country _____

Least densely populated country _____

Largest dependent territory or overseas region _____

Smallest dependent territory or overseas region _____

Most populous dependent territory or overseas region _____

Map It!

On the political map of South America, label each independent country and its capital. Then use colored pencils to make each country a different color than the countries that border it.

South America

Map It!

Use this worksheet to organize your information as you research the following geographical features of South America. This will help you be aware of the locations of all the items you will map before you actually begin so that you can use the space well. Finally, mark each item on the physical map of the continent.

South America's major landforms (e.g., mountain ranges, plains, plateaus) _____
_____
_____
_____

South America's major rivers and river basins _____
_____
_____
_____

South America's major inland bodies of water _____
_____
_____

South America's deserts _____
_____
_____

South America's major islands, peninsulas, and capes _____
_____
_____

Bodies of water that border South America _____
_____
_____

South America's highest and lowest points and their elevations _____
_____

Any of the following lines of latitude that intersect South America: Arctic Circle, Tropic of Cancer, Equator, Tropic of Capricorn, Antarctic Circle _____
_____

Any other special geographical features _____
_____
_____

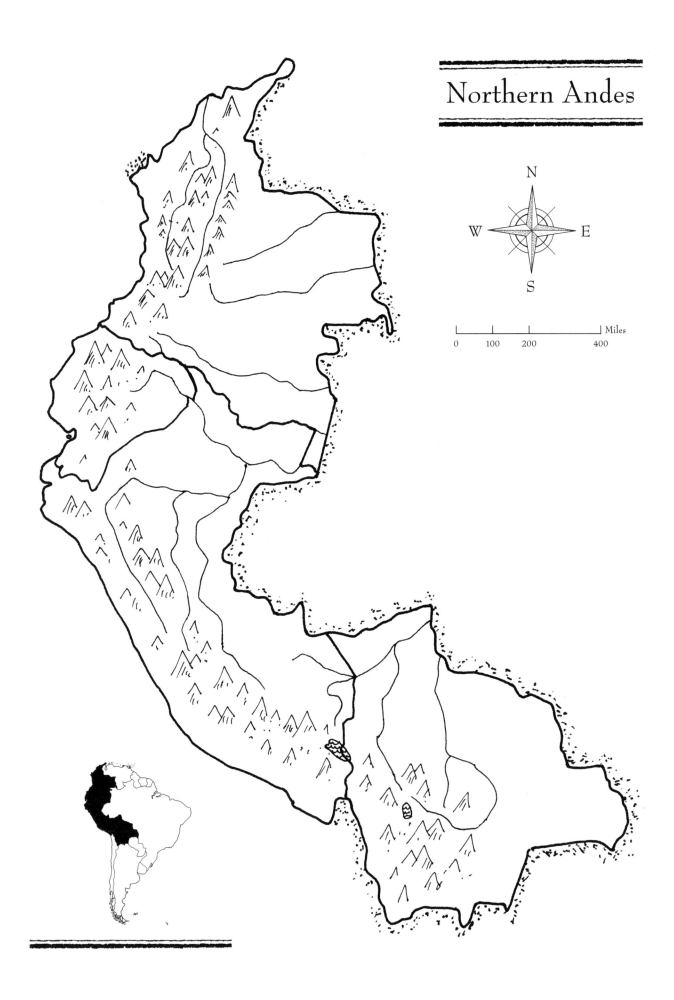

Northern Andes

Map It!

Use this worksheet to organize your information as you research the following geographical features of the Northern Andes. This will help you be aware of the locations of all the items you will map before you actually begin so that you can use the space well. If the region doesn't have one of the features listed, simply write "none" on the blank line. Finally, mark each item on the map of the region.

The name of each independent country and its capital city _____

_____

_____

_____

Five other important cities in the region _____

_____

The region's major landforms (e.g., mountain ranges, plains, plateaus) _____

_____

_____

_____

The region's major rivers and river basins _____

_____

_____

_____

The region's major inland bodies of water _____

_____

_____

The region's deserts _____

_____

The region's important islands, peninsulas, and capes _____

_____

_____

Bodies of water that border the region _____

_____

_____

Any other special geographical features _____

_____

Bolivia

Gather these facts about Bolivia, filling in the blanks.

Capital _____ Type of government _____

Date of independence _____ From _____

Chief of state _____

Head of government _____

Name for citizen (e.g., Canadian) _____

Current population _____ World rank in population _____

Life expectancy _____ men _____ women Literacy _____ % male _____ % female

Ethnic groups _____

Major religions _____

Major languages _____

Land area _____ Water area _____ World rank in area _____

Five largest cities and their populations _____

_____

Bordering nations _____

_____

Climate _____

Terrain _____

Highest point and its elevation _____

Lowest point and its elevation _____

GDP _____ Per capita GDP _____ World rank in GDP _____

Major natural resources _____

Major industries _____

Chief agricultural products _____

Major exports _____

Major imports _____

Colombia

Gather these facts about Colombia, filling in the blanks.

Capital _____ Type of government _____

Date of independence _____ From _____

Chief of state _____

Head of government _____

Name for citizen (e.g., Canadian) _____

Current population _____ World rank in population _____

Life expectancy _____ men _____ women Literacy _____ % male _____ % female

Ethnic groups _____

Major religions _____

Major languages _____

Land area _____ Water area _____ World rank in area _____

Five largest cities and their populations _____

_____

Bordering nations _____

_____

Climate _____

Terrain _____

Highest point and its elevation _____

Lowest point and its elevation _____

GDP _____ Per capita GDP _____ World rank in GDP _____

Major natural resources _____

Major industries _____

Chief agricultural products _____

Major exports _____

Major imports _____

Ecuador

Gather these facts about Ecuador, filling in the blanks.

Capital _____ Type of government _____

Date of independence _____ From _____

Chief of state _____

Head of government _____

Name for citizen (e.g., Canadian) _____

Current population _____ World rank in population _____

Life expectancy _____ men _____ women   Literacy _____ % male _____ % female

Ethnic groups _____

Major religions _____

Major languages _____

Land area _____ Water area _____ World rank in area _____

Five largest cities and their populations _____

_____

Bordering nations _____

_____

Climate _____

Terrain _____

Highest point and its elevation _____

Lowest point and its elevation _____

GDP _____ Per capita GDP _____ World rank in GDP _____

Major natural resources _____

Major industries _____

Chief agricultural products _____

Major exports _____

Major imports _____

Peru

Gather these facts about Peru, filling in the blanks.

Capital _____ Type of government _____

Date of independence _____ From _____

Chief of state _____

Head of government _____

Name for citizen (e.g., Canadian) _____

Current population _____ World rank in population _____

Life expectancy _____ men _____ women   Literacy _____ % male _____ % female

Ethnic groups _____

Major religions _____

Major languages _____

Land area _____ Water area _____ World rank in area _____

Five largest cities and their populations _____

_____

Bordering nations _____

_____

Climate _____

Terrain _____

Highest point and its elevation _____

Lowest point and its elevation _____

GDP _____ Per capita GDP _____ World rank in GDP _____

Major natural resources _____

Major industries _____

Chief agricultural products _____

Major exports _____

Major imports _____

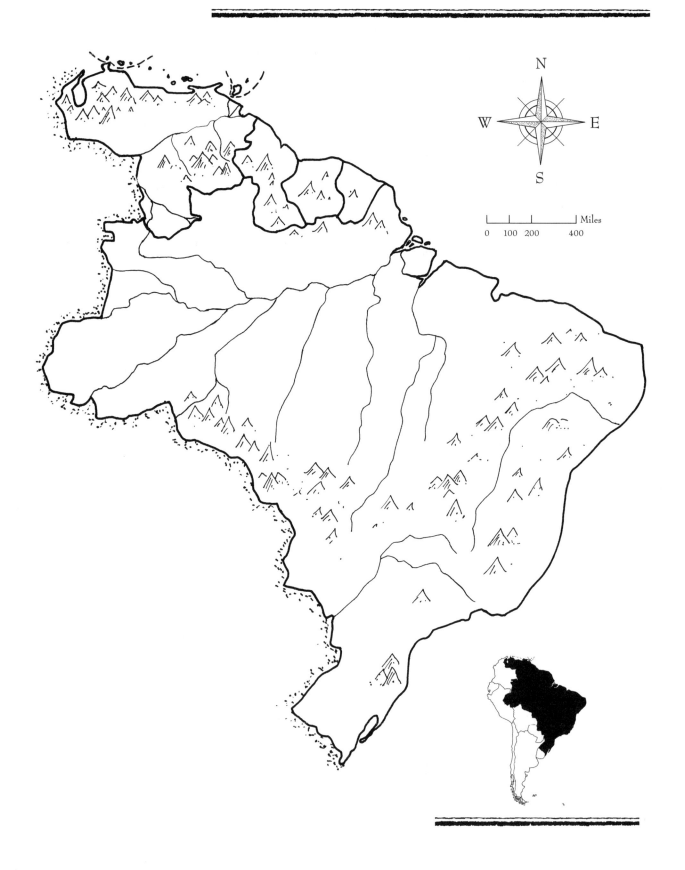

Map It!

Use this worksheet to organize your information as you research the following geographical features of Northern South America and Brazil. This will help you be aware of the locations of all the items you will map before you actually begin so that you can use the space well. If the region doesn't have one of the features listed, simply write "none" on the blank line. Finally, mark each item on the map of the region.

The name of each independent country and its capital city _____

_____

_____

_____

Five other important cities in the region _____

_____

The region's major landforms (e.g., mountain ranges, plains, plateaus) _____

_____

_____

_____

The region's major rivers and river basins _____

_____

_____

_____

The region's major inland bodies of water _____

_____

_____

The region's deserts _____

_____

The region's important islands, peninsulas, and capes _____

_____

_____

Bodies of water that border the region _____

_____

_____

Any other special geographical features _____

_____

Brazil

Gather these facts about Brazil, filling in the blanks.

Capital _____ Type of government _____

Date of independence _____ From _____

Chief of state _____

Head of government _____

Name for citizen (e.g., Canadian) _____

Current population _____ World rank in population _____

Life expectancy _____ men _____ women Literacy _____ % male _____ % female

Ethnic groups _____

Major religions _____

Major languages _____

Land area _____ Water area _____ World rank in area _____

Five largest cities and their populations _____

_____

Bordering nations _____

_____

Climate _____

Terrain _____

Highest point and its elevation _____

Lowest point and its elevation _____

GDP _____ Per capita GDP _____ World rank in GDP _____

Major natural resources _____

Major industries _____

Chief agricultural products _____

Major exports _____

Major imports _____

Guyana

Gather these facts about Guyana, filling in the blanks.

Capital _____ Type of government _____

Date of independence _____ From _____

Chief of state _____

Head of government _____

Name for citizen (e.g., Canadian) _____

Current population _____ World rank in population _____

Life expectancy _____ men _____ women Literacy _____ % male _____ % female

Ethnic groups _____

Major religions _____

Major languages _____

Land area _____ Water area _____ World rank in area _____

Five largest cities and their populations _____

_____

Bordering nations _____

_____

Climate _____

Terrain _____

Highest point and its elevation _____

Lowest point and its elevation _____

GDP _____ Per capita GDP _____ World rank in GDP _____

Major natural resources _____

Major industries _____

Chief agricultural products _____

Major exports _____

Major imports _____

Suriname

Gather these facts about Suriname, filling in the blanks.

Capital _____ Type of government _____

Date of independence _____ From _____

Chief of state _____

Head of government _____

Name for citizen (e.g., Canadian) _____

Current population _____ World rank in population _____

Life expectancy _____ men _____ women   Literacy _____ % male _____ % female

Ethnic groups _____

Major religions _____

Major languages _____

Land area _____ Water area _____ World rank in area _____

Five largest cities and their populations _____

_____

Bordering nations _____

_____

Climate _____

Terrain _____

Highest point and its elevation _____

Lowest point and its elevation _____

GDP _____ Per capita GDP _____ World rank in GDP _____

Major natural resources _____

Major industries _____

Chief agricultural products _____

Major exports _____

Major imports _____

Venezuela

Gather these facts about Venezuela, filling in the blanks.

Capital _____ Type of government _____

Date of independence _____ From _____

Chief of state _____

Head of government _____

Name for citizen (e.g., Canadian) _____

Current population _____ World rank in population _____

Life expectancy _____ men _____ women Literacy _____ % male _____ % female

Ethnic groups _____

Major religions _____

Major languages _____

Land area _____ Water area _____ World rank in area _____

Five largest cities and their populations _____

_____

Bordering nations _____

_____

Climate _____

Terrain _____

Highest point and its elevation _____

Lowest point and its elevation _____

GDP _____ Per capita GDP _____ World rank in GDP _____

Major natural resources _____

Major industries _____

Chief agricultural products _____

Major exports _____

Major imports _____

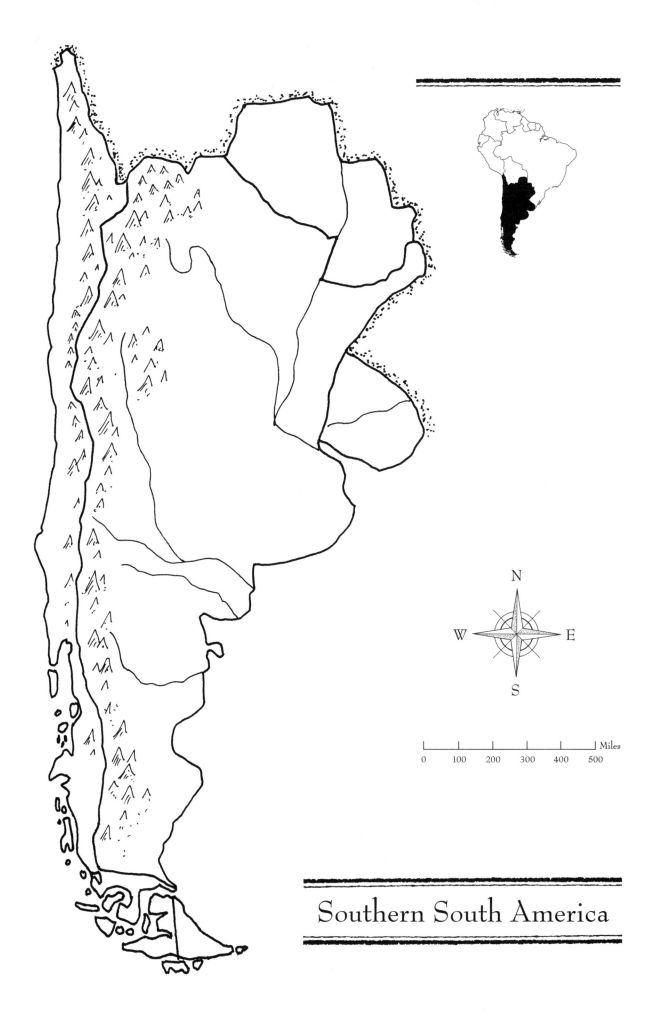

Southern South America

Map It!

Use this worksheet to organize your information as you research the following geographical features of Southern South America. This will help you be aware of the locations of all the items you will map before you actually begin so that you can use the space well. If the region doesn't have one of the features listed, simply write "none" on the blank line. Finally, mark each item on the map of the region.

The name of each independent country and its capital city _____

_____

_____

_____

Five other important cities in the region _____

_____

The region's major landforms (e.g., mountain ranges, plains, plateaus) _____

_____

_____

_____

The region's major rivers and river basins _____

_____

_____

_____

The region's major inland bodies of water _____

_____

_____

The region's deserts _____

_____

The region's important islands, peninsulas, and capes _____

_____

_____

Bodies of water that border the region _____

_____

_____

Any other special geographical features _____

_____

Argentina

Gather these facts about Argentina, filling in the blanks.

Capital _____ Type of government _____

Date of independence _____ From _____

Chief of state _____

Head of government _____

Name for citizen (e.g., Canadian) _____

Current population _____ World rank in population _____

Life expectancy _____ men _____ women   Literacy _____ % male _____ % female

Ethnic groups _____

Major religions _____

Major languages _____

Land area _____ Water area _____ World rank in area _____

Five largest cities and their populations _____

_____

Bordering nations _____

_____

Climate _____

Terrain _____

Highest point and its elevation _____

Lowest point and its elevation _____

GDP _____ Per capita GDP _____ World rank in GDP _____

Major natural resources _____

Major industries _____

Chief agricultural products _____

Major exports _____

Major imports _____

Chile

Gather these facts about Chile, filling in the blanks.

Capital _____ Type of government _____

Date of independence _____ From _____

Chief of state _____

Head of government _____

Name for citizen (e.g., Canadian) _____

Current population _____ World rank in population _____

Life expectancy _____ men _____ women Literacy _____ % male _____ % female

Ethnic groups _____

Major religions _____

Major languages _____

Land area _____ Water area _____ World rank in area _____

Five largest cities and their populations _____

_____

Bordering nations _____

_____

Climate _____

Terrain _____

Highest point and its elevation _____

Lowest point and its elevation _____

GDP _____ Per capita GDP _____ World rank in GDP _____

Major natural resources _____

Major industries _____

Chief agricultural products _____

Major exports _____

Major imports _____

Paraguay

Gather these facts about Paraguay, filling in the blanks.

Capital _____ Type of government _____

Date of independence _____ From _____

Chief of state _____

Head of government _____

Name for citizen (e.g., Canadian) _____

Current population _____ World rank in population _____

Life expectancy _____ men _____ women   Literacy _____ % male _____ % female

Ethnic groups _____

Major religions _____

Major languages _____

Land area _____ Water area _____ World rank in area _____

Five largest cities and their populations _____

_____

Bordering nations _____

_____

Climate _____

Terrain _____

Highest point and its elevation _____

Lowest point and its elevation _____

GDP _____ Per capita GDP _____ World rank in GDP _____

Major natural resources _____

Major industries _____

Chief agricultural products _____

Major exports _____

Major imports _____

Uruguay

Gather these facts about Uruguay, filling in the blanks.

Capital _____ Type of government _____

Date of independence _____ From _____

Chief of state _____

Head of government _____

Name for citizen (e.g., Canadian) _____

Current population _____ World rank in population _____

Life expectancy _____ men _____ women Literacy _____ % male _____ % female

Ethnic groups _____

Major religions _____

Major languages _____

Land area _____ Water area _____ World rank in area _____

Five largest cities and their populations _____

_____

Bordering nations _____

_____

Climate _____

Terrain _____

Highest point and its elevation _____

Lowest point and its elevation _____

GDP _____ Per capita GDP _____ World rank in GDP _____

Major natural resources _____

Major industries _____

Chief agricultural products _____

Major exports _____

Major imports _____

Africa

Africa

Africa

Gather these facts about the continent of Africa, filling in the blanks.

Total land area _____ Rank in area _____ of 7

Total population _____ Rank in population _____ of 7

Major languages _____ _____

Major religions _____

Major natural resources _____

Longest river _____

Highest mountain _____

Lowest point _____

Largest lake _____

Biggest desert _____

Biggest island _____

Three largest cities _____

Number of independent countries _____

Largest country _____

Smallest country _____

Most populous country _____

Least populous country _____

Most densely populated country _____

Least densely populated country _____

Largest dependent territory or overseas region _____

Smallest dependent territory or overseas region _____

Most populous dependent territory or overseas region _____

Map It!

On the political map of Africa, label each independent country and its capital. Then use colored pencils to make each country a different color than the countries that border it.

Africa

Map It!

Use this worksheet to organize your information as you research the following geographical features of Africa. This will help you be aware of the locations of all the items you will map before you actually begin so that you can use the space well. Finally, mark each item on the physical map of the continent.

Africa's major landforms (e.g., mountain ranges, plains, plateaus) _____

_____

_____

_____

Africa's major rivers and river basins _____

_____

_____

_____

Africa's major inland bodies of water _____

_____

_____

Africa's deserts _____

_____

_____

Africa's major islands, peninsulas, and capes _____

_____

_____

Bodies of water that border Africa _____

_____

_____

Africa's highest and lowest points and their elevations _____

_____

Any of the following lines of latitude that intersect Africa: Arctic Circle, Tropic of Cancer, Equator, Tropic of Capricorn, Antarctic Circle _____

_____

Any other special geographical features _____

_____

_____

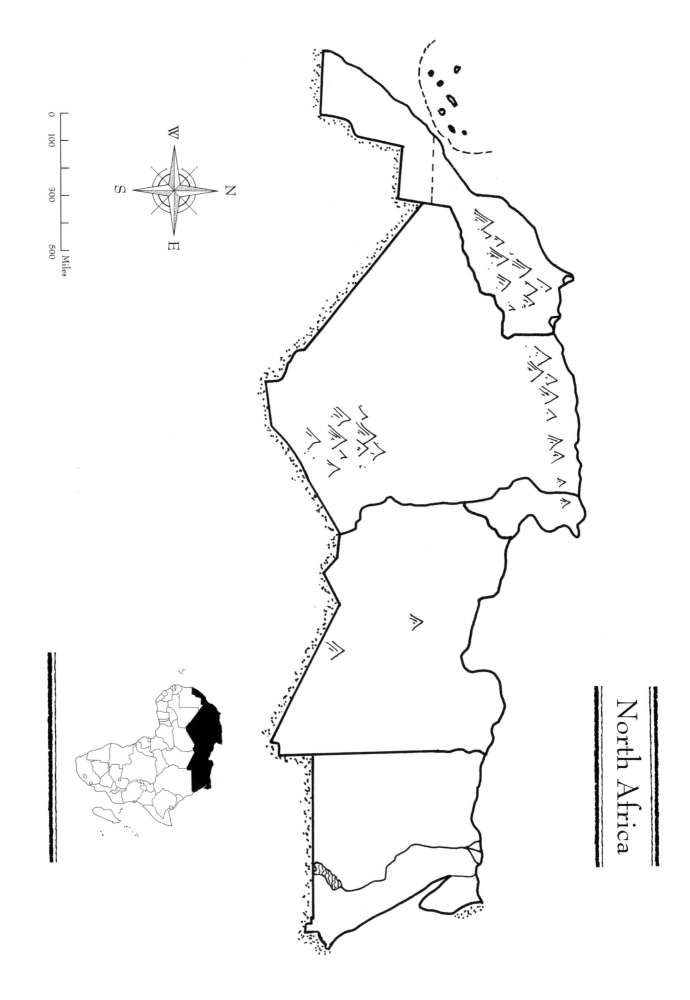

North Africa

Map It!

Use this worksheet to organize your information as you research the following geographical features of North Africa. This will help you be aware of the locations of all the items you will map before you actually begin so that you can use the space well. If the region doesn't have one of the features listed, simply write "none" on the blank line. Finally, mark each item on the map of the region.

The name of each independent country and its capital city _____

_____

_____

_____

Five other important cities in the region _____

_____

The region's major landforms (e.g., mountain ranges, plains, plateaus) _____

_____

_____

_____

The region's major rivers and river basins _____

_____

_____

_____

The region's major inland bodies of water _____

_____

_____

The region's deserts _____

_____

The region's important islands, peninsulas, and capes _____

_____

_____

Bodies of water that border the region _____

_____

_____

Any other special geographical features _____

_____

Algeria

Gather these facts about Algeria, filling in the blanks.

Capital _____ Type of government _____

Date of independence _____ From _____

Chief of state _____

Head of government _____

Name for citizen (e.g., Canadian) _____

Current population _____ World rank in population _____

Life expectancy _____ men _____ women Literacy _____ % male _____ % female

Ethnic groups _____

Major religions _____

Major languages _____

Land area _____ Water area _____ World rank in area _____

Five largest cities and their populations _____

_____

Bordering nations _____

_____

Climate _____

Terrain _____

Highest point and its elevation _____

Lowest point and its elevation _____

GDP_____ Per capita GDP _____ World rank in GDP _____

Major natural resources _____

Major industries _____

Chief agricultural products _____

Major exports _____

Major imports _____

Egypt

Gather these facts about Egypt, filling in the blanks.

Capital _____ Type of government _____

Date of independence _____ From _____

Chief of state _____

Head of government _____

Name for citizen (e.g., Canadian) _____

Current population _____ World rank in population _____

Life expectancy _____ men _____ women Literacy _____ % male _____ % female

Ethnic groups _____

Major religions _____

Major languages _____

Land area _____ Water area _____ World rank in area _____

Five largest cities and their populations _____

_____

Bordering nations _____

_____

Climate _____

Terrain _____

Highest point and its elevation _____

Lowest point and its elevation _____

GDP _____ Per capita GDP _____ World rank in GDP _____

Major natural resources _____

Major industries _____

Chief agricultural products _____

Major exports _____

Major imports _____

Libya

Gather these facts about Libya, filling in the blanks.

Capital _____ Type of government _____

Date of independence _____ From _____

Chief of state _____

Head of government _____

Name for citizen (e.g., Canadian) _____

Current population _____ World rank in population _____

Life expectancy _____ men _____ women Literacy _____ % male _____ % female

Ethnic groups _____

Major religions _____

Major languages _____

Land area _____ Water area _____ World rank in area _____

Five largest cities and their populations _____

_____

Bordering nations _____

_____

Climate _____

Terrain _____

Highest point and its elevation _____

Lowest point and its elevation _____

GDP _____ Per capita GDP _____ World rank in GDP _____

Major natural resources _____

Major industries _____

Chief agricultural products _____

Major exports _____

Major imports _____

Morocco

Gather these facts about Morocco, filling in the blanks.

Capital _____ Type of government _____

Date of independence _____ From _____

Chief of state _____

Head of government _____

Name for citizen (e.g., Canadian) _____

Current population _____ World rank in population _____

Life expectancy _____ men _____ women   Literacy _____ % male _____ % female

Ethnic groups _____

Major religions _____

Major languages _____

Land area _____ Water area _____ World rank in area _____

Five largest cities and their populations _____

_____

Bordering nations _____

_____

Climate _____

Terrain _____

Highest point and its elevation _____

Lowest point and its elevation _____

GDP _____ Per capita GDP _____ World rank in GDP _____

Major natural resources _____

Major industries _____

Chief agricultural products _____

Major exports _____

Major imports _____

Tunisia

Gather these facts about Tunisia, filling in the blanks.

Capital _____ Type of government _____

Date of independence _____ From _____

Chief of state _____

Head of government _____

Name for citizen (e.g., Canadian) _____

Current population _____ World rank in population _____

Life expectancy _____ men _____ women Literacy _____ % male _____ % female

Ethnic groups _____

Major religions _____

Major languages _____

Land area _____ Water area _____ World rank in area _____

Five largest cities and their populations _____

_____

Bordering nations _____

_____

Climate _____

Terrain _____

Highest point and its elevation _____

Lowest point and its elevation _____

GDP _____ Per capita GDP _____ World rank in GDP _____

Major natural resources _____

Major industries _____

Chief agricultural products _____

Major exports _____

Major imports _____

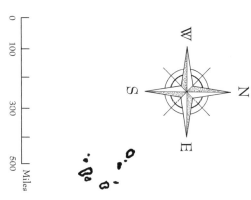

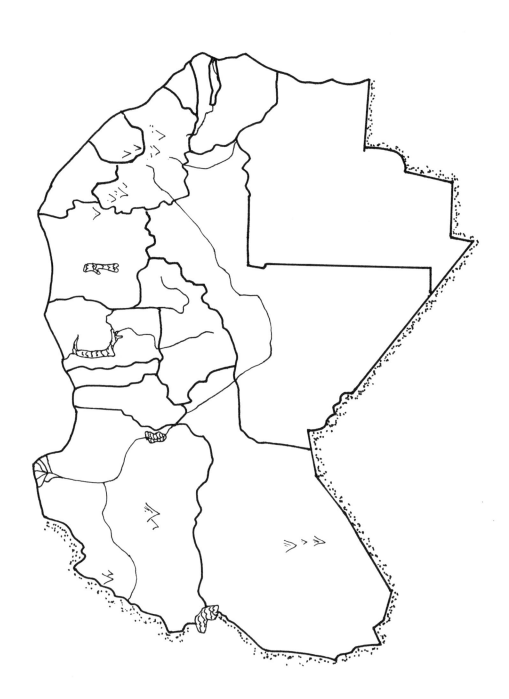

Map It!

Use this worksheet to organize your information as you research the following geographical features of West Africa. This will help you be aware of the locations of all the items you will map before you actually begin so that you can use the space well. If the region doesn't have one of the features listed, simply write "none" on the blank line. Finally, mark each item on the map of the region.

The name of each independent country and its capital city _____

_____

_____

_____

_____

_____

The region's major landforms (e.g., mountain ranges, plains, plateaus) _____

_____

_____

_____

The region's major rivers and river basins _____

_____

_____

_____

The region's major inland bodies of water _____

_____

_____

The region's deserts _____

_____

The region's important islands, peninsulas, and capes _____

_____

_____

Bodies of water that border the region _____

_____

_____

Any other special geographical features _____

_____

Benin

Gather these facts about Benin, filling in the blanks.

Capital _____ Type of government _____

Date of independence _____ From _____

Chief of state _____

Head of government _____

Name for citizen (e.g., Canadian) _____

Current population _____ World rank in population _____

Life expectancy _____ men _____ women Literacy _____ % male _____ % female

Ethnic groups _____

Major religions _____

Major languages _____

Land area _____ Water area _____ World rank in area _____

Five largest cities and their populations _____

_____

Bordering nations _____

_____

Climate _____

Terrain _____

Highest point and its elevation _____

Lowest point and its elevation _____

GDP _____ Per capita GDP _____ World rank in GDP _____

Major natural resources _____

Major industries _____

Chief agricultural products _____

Major exports _____

Major imports _____

Burkina Faso

Gather these facts about Burkina Faso, filling in the blanks.

Capital _____ Type of government _____

Date of independence _____ From _____

Chief of state _____

Head of government _____

Name for citizen (e.g., Canadian) _____

Current population _____ World rank in population _____

Life expectancy _____ men _____ women   Literacy _____ % male _____ % female

Ethnic groups _____

Major religions _____

Major languages _____

Land area _____ Water area _____ World rank in area _____

Five largest cities and their populations _____

_____

Bordering nations _____

_____

Climate _____

Terrain _____

Highest point and its elevation _____

Lowest point and its elevation _____

GDP _____ Per capita GDP _____ World rank in GDP _____

Major natural resources _____

Major industries _____

Chief agricultural products _____

Major exports _____

Major imports _____

Cape Verde

Gather these facts about Cape Verde, filling in the blanks.

Capital _____ Type of government _____

Date of independence _____ From _____

Chief of state _____

Head of government _____

Name for citizen (e.g., Canadian) _____

Current population _____ World rank in population _____

Life expectancy _____ men _____ women   Literacy _____ % male _____ % female

Ethnic groups _____

Major religions _____

Major languages _____

Land area _____ Water area _____ World rank in area _____

Five largest cities and their populations _____

_____

Bordering nations _____

_____

Climate _____

Terrain _____

Highest point and its elevation _____

Lowest point and its elevation _____

GDP _____ Per capita GDP _____ World rank in GDP _____

Major natural resources _____

Major industries _____

Chief agricultural products _____

Major exports _____

Major imports _____

Cote d'Ivoire

Gather these facts about Cote d'Ivoire, filling in the blanks.

Capital _____ Type of government _____

Date of independence _____ From _____

Chief of state _____

Head of government _____

Name for citizen (e.g., Canadian) _____

Current population _____ World rank in population _____

Life expectancy _____ men _____ women   Literacy _____ % male _____ % female

Ethnic groups _____

Major religions _____

Major languages _____

Land area _____ Water area _____ World rank in area _____

Five largest cities and their populations _____

_____

Bordering nations _____

_____

Climate _____

Terrain _____

Highest point and its elevation _____

Lowest point and its elevation _____

GDP _____ Per capita GDP _____ World rank in GDP _____

Major natural resources _____

Major industries _____

Chief agricultural products _____

Major exports _____

Major imports _____

The Gambia

Gather these facts about The Gambia, filling in the blanks.

Capital _____ Type of government _____

Date of independence _____ From _____

Chief of state _____

Head of government _____

Name for citizen (e.g., Canadian) _____

Current population _____ World rank in population _____

Life expectancy _____ men _____ women   Literacy _____ % male _____ % female

Ethnic groups _____

Major religions _____

Major languages _____

Land area _____ Water area _____ World rank in area _____

Five largest cities and their populations _____

_____

Bordering nations _____

_____

Climate _____

Terrain _____

Highest point and its elevation _____

Lowest point and its elevation _____

GDP_____ Per capita GDP _____ World rank in GDP _____

Major natural resources _____

Major industries _____

Chief agricultural products _____

Major exports _____

Major imports _____

Ghana

Gather these facts about Ghana, filling in the blanks.

Capital _____ Type of government _____

Date of independence _____ From _____

Chief of state _____

Head of government _____

Name for citizen (e.g., Canadian) _____

Current population _____ World rank in population _____

Life expectancy_____ men _____ women   Literacy_____ % male _____ % female

Ethnic groups _____

Major religions _____

Major languages _____

Land area _____ Water area _____ World rank in area _____

Five largest cities and their populations _____

_____

Bordering nations _____

_____

Climate _____

Terrain _____

Highest point and its elevation _____

Lowest point and its elevation _____

GDP _____ Per capita GDP _____ World rank in GDP _____

Major natural resources _____

Major industries _____

Chief agricultural products _____

Major exports _____

Major imports _____

Guinea

Gather these facts about Guinea, filling in the blanks.

Capital _____ Type of government _____

Date of independence _____ From _____

Chief of state _____

Head of government _____

Name for citizen (e.g., Canadian) _____

Current population _____ World rank in population _____

Life expectancy _____ men _____ women Literacy _____ % male _____ % female

Ethnic groups _____

Major religions _____

Major languages _____

Land area _____ Water area _____ World rank in area _____

Five largest cities and their populations _____

_____

Bordering nations _____

_____

Climate _____

Terrain _____

Highest point and its elevation _____

Lowest point and its elevation _____

GDP _____ Per capita GDP _____ World rank in GDP _____

Major natural resources _____

Major industries _____

Chief agricultural products _____

Major exports _____

Major imports _____

Guinea-Bissau

Gather these facts about Guinea-Bissau, filling in the blanks.

Capital _____ Type of government _____

Date of independence _____ From _____

Chief of state _____

Head of government _____

Name for citizen (e.g., Canadian) _____

Current population _____ World rank in population _____

Life expectancy _____ men _____ women   Literacy _____ % male _____ % female

Ethnic groups _____

Major religions _____

Major languages _____

Land area _____ Water area _____ World rank in area _____

Five largest cities and their populations _____

_____

Bordering nations _____

_____

Climate _____

Terrain _____

Highest point and its elevation _____

Lowest point and its elevation _____

GDP _____ Per capita GDP _____ World rank in GDP _____

Major natural resources _____

Major industries _____

Chief agricultural products _____

Major exports _____

Major imports _____

Liberia

Gather these facts about Liberia, filling in the blanks.

Capital _____ Type of government _____

Date of independence _____ From _____

Chief of state _____

Head of government _____

Name for citizen (e.g., Canadian) _____

Current population _____ World rank in population _____

Life expectancy _____ men _____ women Literacy _____ % male _____ % female

Ethnic groups _____

Major religions _____

Major languages _____

Land area _____ Water area _____ World rank in area _____

Five largest cities and their populations _____

_____

Bordering nations _____

_____

Climate _____

Terrain _____

Highest point and its elevation _____

Lowest point and its elevation _____

GDP _____ Per capita GDP _____ World rank in GDP _____

Major natural resources _____

Major industries _____

Chief agricultural products _____

Major exports _____

Major imports _____

Mali

Gather these facts about Mali, filling in the blanks.

Capital _____ Type of government _____

Date of independence _____ From _____

Chief of state _____

Head of government _____

Name for citizen (e.g., Canadian) _____

Current population _____ World rank in population _____

Life expectancy _____ men _____ women Literacy _____ % male _____ % female

Ethnic groups _____

Major religions _____

Major languages _____

Land area _____ Water area _____ World rank in area _____

Five largest cities and their populations _____

_____

Bordering nations _____

_____

Climate _____

Terrain _____

Highest point and its elevation _____

Lowest point and its elevation _____

GDP _____ Per capita GDP _____ World rank in GDP _____

Major natural resources _____

Major industries _____

Chief agricultural products _____

Major exports _____

Major imports _____

Mauritania

Gather these facts about Mauritania, filling in the blanks.

Capital _____ Type of government _____

Date of independence _____ From _____

Chief of state _____

Head of government _____

Name for citizen (e.g., Canadian) _____

Current population _____ World rank in population _____

Life expectancy _____ men _____ women Literacy _____ % male _____ % female

Ethnic groups _____

Major religions _____

Major languages _____

Land area _____ Water area _____ World rank in area _____

Five largest cities and their populations _____

_____

Bordering nations _____

_____

Climate _____

Terrain _____

Highest point and its elevation _____

Lowest point and its elevation _____

GDP _____ Per capita GDP _____ World rank in GDP _____

Major natural resources _____

Major industries _____

Chief agricultural products _____

Major exports _____

Major imports _____

Niger

Gather these facts about Niger, filling in the blanks.

Capital _____ Type of government _____

Date of independence _____ From _____

Chief of state _____

Head of government _____

Name for citizen (e.g., Canadian) _____

Current population _____ World rank in population _____

Life expectancy _____ men _____ women Literacy _____ % male _____ % female

Ethnic groups _____

Major religions _____

Major languages _____

Land area _____ Water area _____ World rank in area _____

Five largest cities and their populations _____

_____

Bordering nations _____

_____

Climate _____

Terrain _____

Highest point and its elevation _____

Lowest point and its elevation _____

GDP _____ Per capita GDP _____ World rank in GDP _____

Major natural resources _____

Major industries _____

Chief agricultural products _____

Major exports _____

Major imports _____

Nigeria

Gather these facts about Nigeria, filling in the blanks.

Capital _____ Type of government _____

Date of independence _____ From _____

Chief of state _____

Head of government _____

Name for citizen (e.g., Canadian) _____

Current population _____ World rank in population _____

Life expectancy _____ men _____ women   Literacy _____ % male _____ % female

Ethnic groups _____

Major religions _____

Major languages _____

Land area _____ Water area _____ World rank in area _____

Five largest cities and their populations _____

_____

Bordering nations _____

_____

Climate _____

Terrain _____

Highest point and its elevation _____

Lowest point and its elevation _____

GDP _____ Per capita GDP _____ World rank in GDP _____

Major natural resources _____

Major industries _____

Chief agricultural products _____

Major exports _____

Major imports _____

Senegal

Gather these facts about Senegal, filling in the blanks.

Capital _____ Type of government _____

Date of independence _____ From _____

Chief of state _____

Head of government _____

Name for citizen (e.g., Canadian) _____

Current population _____ World rank in population _____

Life expectancy _____ men _____ women   Literacy _____ % male _____ % female

Ethnic groups _____

Major religions _____

Major languages _____

Land area _____ Water area _____ World rank in area _____

Five largest cities and their populations _____

_____

Bordering nations _____

_____

Climate _____

Terrain _____

Highest point and its elevation _____

Lowest point and its elevation _____

GDP _____ Per capita GDP _____ World rank in GDP _____

Major natural resources _____

Major industries _____

Chief agricultural products _____

Major exports _____

Major imports _____

Sierra Leone

Gather these facts about Sierra Leone, filling in the blanks.

Capital _____ Type of government _____

Date of independence _____ From _____

Chief of state _____

Head of government _____

Name for citizen (e.g., Canadian) _____

Current population _____ World rank in population _____

Life expectancy_____ men _____ women   Literacy_____ % male _____ % female

Ethnic groups _____

Major religions _____

Major languages _____

Land area _____ Water area _____ World rank in area _____

Five largest cities and their populations _____

_____

Bordering nations _____

_____

Climate _____

Terrain _____

Highest point and its elevation _____

Lowest point and its elevation _____

GDP_____ Per capita GDP _____ World rank in GDP _____

Major natural resources _____

Major industries _____

Chief agricultural products _____

Major exports _____

Major imports _____

Togo

Gather these facts about Togo, filling in the blanks.

Capital _____ Type of government _____

Date of independence _____ From _____

Chief of state _____ _____

Head of government _____

Name for citizen (e.g., Canadian) _____

Current population _____ World rank in population _____

Life expectancy _____ men _____ women   Literacy _____ % male _____ % female

Ethnic groups _____

Major religions _____

Major languages _____

Land area _____ Water area _____ World rank in area _____

Five largest cities and their populations _____

_____

Bordering nations _____

_____

Climate _____

Terrain _____

Highest point and its elevation _____

Lowest point and its elevation _____

GDP _____ Per capita GDP _____ World rank in GDP _____

Major natural resources _____

Major industries _____

Chief agricultural products _____

Major exports _____

Major imports _____

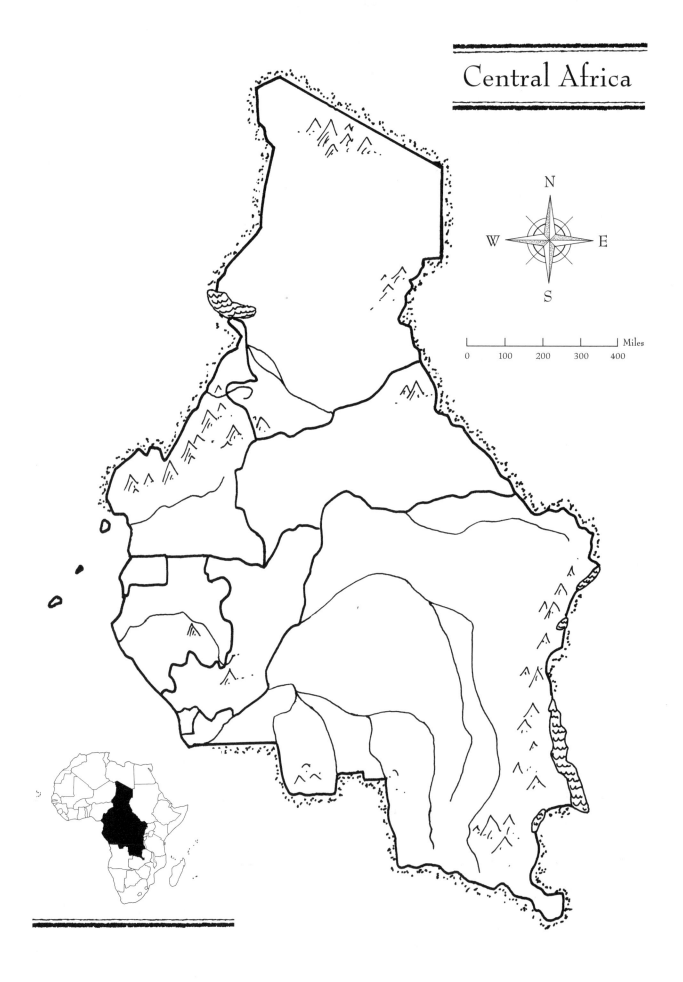

Central Africa

Map It!

Use this worksheet to organize your information as you research the following geographical features of Central Africa. This will help you be aware of the locations of all the items you will map before you actually begin so that you can use the space well. If the region doesn't have one of the features listed, simply write "none" on the blank line. Finally, mark each item on the map of the region.

The name of each independent country and its capital city _____

_____

_____

_____

Five other important cities in the region _____

_____

The region's major landforms (e.g., mountain ranges, plains, plateaus) _____

_____

_____

_____

The region's major rivers and river basins _____

_____

_____

_____

The region's major inland bodies of water _____

_____

_____

The region's deserts _____

_____

The region's important islands, peninsulas, and capes _____

_____

_____

Bodies of water that border the region _____

_____

_____

Any other special geographical features _____

_____

Cameroon

Gather these facts about Cameroon, filling in the blanks.

Capital _____ Type of government _____

Date of independence _____ From _____

Chief of state _____

Head of government _____

Name for citizen (e.g., Canadian) _____

Current population _____ World rank in population _____

Life expectancy _____ men _____ women Literacy _____ % male _____ % female

Ethnic groups _____

Major religions _____

Major languages _____

Land area _____ Water area _____ World rank in area _____

Five largest cities and their populations _____

_____

Bordering nations _____

_____

Climate _____

Terrain _____

Highest point and its elevation _____

Lowest point and its elevation _____

GDP _____ Per capita GDP _____ World rank in GDP _____

Major natural resources _____

Major industries _____

Chief agricultural products _____

Major exports _____

Major imports _____

Central African Republic

Gather these facts about the Central African Republic, filling in the blanks.

Capital _____ Type of government _____

Date of independence _____ From _____

Chief of state _____

Head of government _____

Name for citizen (e.g., Canadian) _____

Current population _____ World rank in population _____

Life expectancy _____ men _____ women Literacy _____ % male _____ % female

Ethnic groups _____

Major religions _____

Major languages _____

Land area _____ Water area _____ World rank in area _____

Five largest cities and their populations _____

_____

Bordering nations _____

_____

Climate _____

Terrain _____

Highest point and its elevation _____

Lowest point and its elevation _____

GDP _____ Per capita GDP _____ World rank in GDP _____

Major natural resources _____

Major industries _____

Chief agricultural products _____

Major exports _____

Major imports _____

Chad

Gather these facts about Chad, filling in the blanks.

Capital _____ Type of government _____

Date of independence _____ From _____

Chief of state _____

Head of government _____

Name for citizen (e.g., Canadian) _____

Current population _____ World rank in population _____

Life expectancy _____ men _____ women Literacy _____ % male _____ % female

Ethnic groups _____

Major religions _____

Major languages _____

Land area _____ Water area _____ World rank in area _____

Five largest cities and their populations _____

_____

Bordering nations _____

_____

Climate _____

Terrain _____

Highest point and its elevation _____

Lowest point and its elevation _____

GDP _____ Per capita GDP _____ World rank in GDP _____

Major natural resources _____

Major industries _____

Chief agricultural products _____

Major exports _____

Major imports _____

Republic of the Congo

Gather these facts about the Republic of the Congo, filling in the blanks.

Capital _____ Type of government _____

Date of independence _____ From _____

Chief of state _____

Head of government _____

Name for citizen (e.g., Canadian) _____

Current population _____ World rank in population _____

Life expectancy _____ men _____ women Literacy _____ % male _____ % female

Ethnic groups _____

Major religions _____

Major languages _____

Land area _____ Water area _____ World rank in area _____

Five largest cities and their populations _____

_____

Bordering nations _____

_____

Climate _____

Terrain _____

Highest point and its elevation _____

Lowest point and its elevation _____

GDP _____ Per capita GDP _____ World rank in GDP _____

Major natural resources _____

Major industries _____

Chief agricultural products _____

Major exports _____

Major imports _____

Democratic Republic of the Congo

Gather these facts about the Democratic Republic of the Congo, filling in the blanks.

Capital _____ Type of government _____ _____

Date of independence _____ From _____

Chief of state _____

Head of government _____

Name for citizen (e.g., Canadian) _____

Current population _____ World rank in population _____

Life expectancy _____ men _____ women Literacy _____ % male _____ % female

Ethnic groups _____

Major religions _____

Major languages _____

Land area _____ Water area _____ World rank in area _____

Five largest cities and their populations _____

_____

Bordering nations _____

_____

Climate _____

Terrain _____

Highest point and its elevation _____

Lowest point and its elevation _____

GDP _____ Per capita GDP _____ World rank in GDP _____

Major natural resources _____

Major industries _____

Chief agricultural products _____

Major exports _____

Major imports _____

Equatorial Guinea

Gather these facts about Equatorial Guinea, filling in the blanks.

Capital _____ Type of government _____

Date of independence _____ From _____

Chief of state _____ _____ _____

Head of government _____

Name for citizen (e.g., Canadian) _____

Current population _____ World rank in population _____

Life expectancy _____ men _____ women Literacy _____ % male _____ % female

Ethnic groups _____

Major religions _____

Major languages _____

Land area _____ Water area _____ World rank in area _____

Five largest cities and their populations _____

_____

Bordering nations _____

_____

Climate _____

Terrain _____

Highest point and its elevation _____

Lowest point and its elevation _____

GDP _____ Per capita GDP _____ World rank in GDP _____

Major natural resources _____

Major industries _____

Chief agricultural products _____

Major exports _____

Major imports _____

Gabon

Gather these facts about Gabon, filling in the blanks.

Capital _____ Type of government _____

Date of independence _____ From _____

Chief of state _____

Head of government _____

Name for citizen (e.g., Canadian) _____

Current population _____ World rank in population _____

Life expectancy _____ men _____ women Literacy _____ % male _____ % female

Ethnic groups _____

Major religions _____

Major languages _____

Land area _____ Water area _____ World rank in area _____

Five largest cities and their populations _____

_____

Bordering nations _____

_____

Climate _____

Terrain _____

Highest point and its elevation _____

Lowest point and its elevation _____

GDP _____ Per capita GDP _____ World rank in GDP _____

Major natural resources _____

Major industries _____

Chief agricultural products _____

Major exports _____

Major imports _____

Sao Tome and Principe

Gather these facts about Sao Tome and Principe, filling in the blanks.

Capital _____ Type of government _____

Date of independence _____ From _____

Chief of state _____ _____

Head of government _____

Name for citizen (e.g., Canadian) _____

Current population _____ World rank in population _____

Life expectancy _____ men _____ women Literacy _____ % male _____ % female

Ethnic groups _____

Major religions _____

Major languages _____

Land area _____ Water area _____ World rank in area _____

Five largest cities and their populations _____

_____

Bordering nations _____

_____

Climate _____

Terrain _____

Highest point and its elevation _____

Lowest point and its elevation _____

GDP _____ Per capita GDP _____ World rank in GDP _____

Major natural resources _____

Major industries _____

Chief agricultural products _____

Major exports _____

Major imports _____

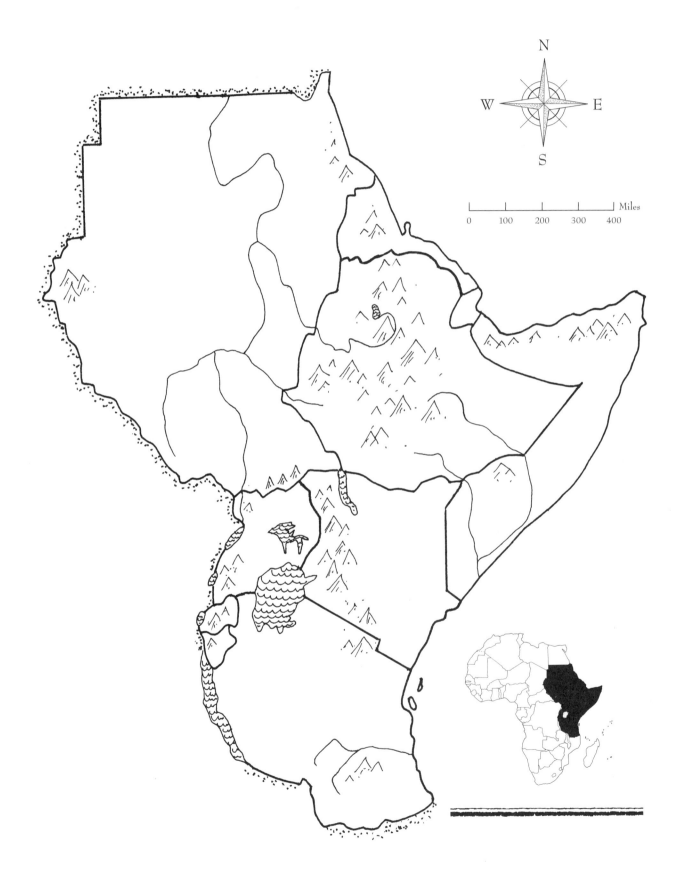

East Africa

Map It!

Use this worksheet to organize your information as you research the following geographical features of East Africa. This will help you be aware of the locations of all the items you will map before you actually begin so that you can use the space well. If the region doesn't have one of the features listed, simply write "none" on the blank line. Finally, mark each item on the map of the region.

The name of each independent country and its capital city _____

_____

_____

_____

_____

_____

The region's major landforms (e.g., mountain ranges, plains, plateaus) _____

_____

_____

_____

The region's major rivers and river basins _____

_____

_____

_____

The region's major inland bodies of water _____

_____

_____

The region's deserts _____

_____

The region's important islands, peninsulas, and capes _____

_____

_____

Bodies of water that border the region _____

_____

_____

Any other special geographical features _____

_____

Burundi

Gather these facts about Burundi, filling in the blanks.

Capital _____ _____ Type of government _____

Date of independence _____ From _____

Chief of state _____

Head of government _____

Name for citizen (e.g., Canadian) _____

Current population _____ World rank in population _____

Life expectancy _____ men _____ women Literacy _____ % male _____ % female

Ethnic groups _____

Major religions _____

Major languages _____

Land area _____ Water area _____ World rank in area _____

Five largest cities and their populations _____

_____

Bordering nations _____

_____

Climate _____

Terrain _____

Highest point and its elevation _____

Lowest point and its elevation _____

GDP _____ Per capita GDP _____ World rank in GDP _____

Major natural resources _____

Major industries _____

Chief agricultural products _____

Major exports _____

Major imports _____

Djibouti

Gather these facts about Djibouti, filling in the blanks.

Capital _____ Type of government _____

Date of independence _____ From _____

Chief of state _____ _____

Head of government _____

Name for citizen (e.g., Canadian) _____

Current population _____ World rank in population _____

Life expectancy _____ men _____ women Literacy _____ % male _____ % female

Ethnic groups _____

Major religions _____

Major languages _____

Land area _____ Water area _____ World rank in area _____

Five largest cities and their populations _____

_____

Bordering nations _____

_____

Climate _____

Terrain _____

Highest point and its elevation _____

Lowest point and its elevation _____

GDP _____ Per capita GDP _____ World rank in GDP _____

Major natural resources _____

Major industries _____

Chief agricultural products _____

Major exports _____

Major imports _____

Eritrea

Gather these facts about Eritrea, filling in the blanks.

Capital _____ _____ Type of government _____

Date of independence _____ From _____

Chief of state _____

Head of government _____

Name for citizen (e.g., Canadian) _____

Current population _____ World rank in population _____

Life expectancy _____ men _____ women   Literacy _____ % male _____ % female

Ethnic groups _____

Major religions _____

Major languages _____

Land area _____ Water area _____ World rank in area _____

Five largest cities and their populations _____

_____

Bordering nations _____

_____

Climate _____

Terrain _____

Highest point and its elevation _____

Lowest point and its elevation _____

GDP _____ Per capita GDP _____ World rank in GDP _____

Major natural resources _____

Major industries _____

Chief agricultural products _____

Major exports _____

Major imports _____

Ethiopia

Gather these facts about Ethiopia, filling in the blanks.

Capital _____ Type of government _____

Date of independence _____ From _____

Chief of state _____

Head of government _____

Name for citizen (e.g., Canadian) _____

Current population _____ World rank in population _____

Life expectancy _____ men _____ women   Literacy _____ % male _____ % female

Ethnic groups _____

Major religions _____

Major languages _____

Land area _____ Water area _____ World rank in area _____

Five largest cities and their populations _____

_____

Bordering nations _____

_____

Climate _____

Terrain _____

Highest point and its elevation _____

Lowest point and its elevation _____

GDP _____ Per capita GDP _____ World rank in GDP _____

Major natural resources _____

Major industries _____

Chief agricultural products _____

Major exports _____

Major imports _____

Kenya

Gather these facts about Kenya, filling in the blanks.

Capital _____ _____ Type of government _____

Date of independence _____ From _____

Chief of state _____

Head of government _____

Name for citizen (e.g., Canadian) _____

Current population _____ World rank in population _____

Life expectancy_____ men _____ women Literacy _____ % male _____ % female

Ethnic groups _____

Major religions _____

Major languages _____

Land area _____ Water area _____ World rank in area _____

Five largest cities and their populations _____

_____

Bordering nations _____

_____

Climate _____

Terrain _____

Highest point and its elevation _____

Lowest point and its elevation _____

GDP_____ Per capita GDP _____ World rank in GDP _____

Major natural resources _____

Major industries _____

Chief agricultural products _____

Major exports _____

Major imports _____

Rwanda

Gather these facts about Rwanda, filling in the blanks.

Capital _____ Type of government _____

Date of independence _____ From _____

Chief of state _____ _____

Head of government _____

Name for citizen (e.g., Canadian) _____

Current population _____ World rank in population _____

Life expectancy _____ men _____ women Literacy _____ % male _____ % female

Ethnic groups _____

Major religions _____

Major languages _____

Land area _____ Water area _____ World rank in area _____

Five largest cities and their populations _____

_____

Bordering nations _____

_____

Climate _____

Terrain _____

Highest point and its elevation _____

Lowest point and its elevation _____

GDP _____ Per capita GDP _____ World rank in GDP _____

Major natural resources _____

Major industries _____

Chief agricultural products _____

Major exports _____

Major imports _____

Somalia

Gather these facts about Somalia, filling in the blanks.

Capital _____ _____ Type of government _____

Date of independence _____ From _____

Chief of state _____

Head of government _____

Name for citizen (e.g., Canadian) _____

Current population _____ World rank in population _____

Life expectancy _____ men _____ women   Literacy _____ % male _____ % female

Ethnic groups _____

Major religions _____

Major languages _____

Land area _____ Water area _____ World rank in area _____

Five largest cities and their populations _____

_____

Bordering nations _____

_____

Climate _____

Terrain _____

Highest point and its elevation _____

Lowest point and its elevation _____

GDP_____ Per capita GDP _____ World rank in GDP _____

Major natural resources _____

Major industries _____

Chief agricultural products _____

Major exports _____

Major imports _____

Sudan

Gather these facts about Sudan, filling in the blanks.

Capital _____ Type of government _____

Date of independence _____ From _____

Chief of state _____ _____

Head of government _____

Name for citizen (e.g., Canadian) _____

Current population _____ World rank in population _____

Life expectancy _____ men _____ women Literacy _____ % male _____ % female

Ethnic groups _____

Major religions _____

Major languages _____

Land area _____ Water area _____ World rank in area _____

Five largest cities and their populations _____

_____

Bordering nations _____

_____

Climate _____

Terrain _____

Highest point and its elevation _____

Lowest point and its elevation _____

GDP _____ Per capita GDP _____ World rank in GDP _____

Major natural resources _____

Major industries _____

Chief agricultural products _____

Major exports _____

Major imports _____

Tanzania

Gather these facts about Tanzania, filling in the blanks.

Capital _____ _____ Type of government _____

Date of independence _____ From _____

Chief of state _____

Head of government _____

Name for citizen (e.g., Canadian) _____

Current population _____ World rank in population _____

Life expectancy _____ men _____ women   Literacy _____ % male _____ % female

Ethnic groups _____

Major religions _____

Major languages _____

Land area _____ Water area _____ World rank in area _____

Five largest cities and their populations _____

_____

Bordering nations _____

_____

Climate _____

Terrain _____

Highest point and its elevation _____

Lowest point and its elevation _____

GDP _____ Per capita GDP _____ World rank in GDP _____

Major natural resources _____

Major industries _____

Chief agricultural products _____

Major exports _____

Major imports _____

Uganda

Gather these facts about Uganda, filling in the blanks.

Capital _____ Type of government _____

Date of independence _____ From _____

Chief of state _____

Head of government _____

Name for citizen (e.g., Canadian) _____

Current population _____ World rank in population _____

Life expectancy _____ men _____ women   Literacy _____ % male _____ % female

Ethnic groups _____

Major religions _____

Major languages _____

Land area _____ Water area _____ World rank in area _____

Five largest cities and their populations _____

_____

Bordering nations _____

_____

Climate _____

Terrain _____

Highest point and its elevation _____

Lowest point and its elevation _____

GDP _____ Per capita GDP _____ World rank in GDP _____

Major natural resources _____

Major industries _____

Chief agricultural products _____

Major exports _____

Major imports _____

Southern Africa

Map It!

Use this worksheet to organize your information as you research the following geographical features of Southern Africa. This will help you be aware of the locations of all the items you will map before you actually begin so that you can use the space well. If the region doesn't have one of the features listed, simply write "none" on the blank line. Finally, mark each item on the map of the region.

The name of each independent country and its capital city _____ _____

_____

_____

_____

_____

_____

The region's major landforms (e.g., mountain ranges, plains, plateaus) _____

_____

_____

The region's major rivers and river basins _____

_____

_____

The region's major inland bodies of water _____

_____

_____

The region's deserts _____

_____

The region's important islands, peninsulas, and capes _____

_____

_____

Bodies of water that border the region _____

_____

_____

Any other special geographical features _____

_____

Angola

Gather these facts about Angola, filling in the blanks.

Capital _____ _____ Type of government _____

Date of independence _____ From _____

Chief of state _____

Head of government _____

Name for citizen (e.g., Canadian) _____

Current population _____ World rank in population _____

Life expectancy _____ men _____ women Literacy _____ % male _____ % female

Ethnic groups _____

Major religions _____

Major languages _____

Land area _____ Water area _____ World rank in area _____

Five largest cities and their populations _____

_____

Bordering nations _____

_____

Climate _____

Terrain _____

Highest point and its elevation _____

Lowest point and its elevation _____

GDP _____ Per capita GDP _____ World rank in GDP _____

Major natural resources _____

Major industries _____

Chief agricultural products _____

Major exports _____

Major imports _____

Botswana

Gather these facts about Botswana, filling in the blanks.

Capital _____ Type of government _____

Date of independence _____ From _____

Chief of state _____ _____

Head of government _____

Name for citizen (e.g., Canadian) _____

Current population _____ World rank in population _____

Life expectancy _____ men _____ women   Literacy _____ % male _____ % female

Ethnic groups _____

Major religions _____

Major languages _____

Land area _____ Water area _____ World rank in area _____

Five largest cities and their populations _____

_____

Bordering nations _____

_____

Climate _____

Terrain _____

Highest point and its elevation _____

Lowest point and its elevation _____

GDP _____ Per capita GDP _____ World rank in GDP _____

Major natural resources _____

Major industries _____

Chief agricultural products _____

Major exports _____

Major imports _____

Comoros

Gather these facts about Comoros, filling in the blanks.

Capital _____ _____ Type of government _____

Date of independence _____ From _____

Chief of state _____

Head of government _____

Name for citizen (e.g., Canadian) _____

Current population _____ World rank in population _____

Life expectancy _____ men _____ women   Literacy _____ % male _____ % female

Ethnic groups _____

Major religions _____

Major languages _____

Land area _____ Water area _____ World rank in area _____

Five largest cities and their populations _____

_____

Bordering nations _____

_____

Climate _____

Terrain _____

Highest point and its elevation _____

Lowest point and its elevation _____

GDP _____ Per capita GDP _____ World rank in GDP _____

Major natural resources _____

Major industries _____

Chief agricultural products _____

Major exports _____

Major imports _____

Lesotho

Gather these facts about Lesotho, filling in the blanks.

Capital _____ Type of government _____

Date of independence _____ From _____

Chief of state _____ ____ _____

Head of government _____

Name for citizen (e.g., Canadian) _____

Current population _____ World rank in population _____

Life expectancy _____ men _____ women Literacy _____ % male _____ % female

Ethnic groups _____

Major religions _____

Major languages _____

Land area _____ Water area _____ World rank in area _____

Five largest cities and their populations _____

_____

Bordering nations _____

_____

Climate _____

Terrain _____

Highest point and its elevation _____

Lowest point and its elevation _____

GDP _____ Per capita GDP _____ World rank in GDP _____

Major natural resources _____

Major industries _____

Chief agricultural products _____

Major exports _____

Major imports _____

Madagascar

Gather these facts about Madagascar, filling in the blanks.

Capital _____ _____ Type of government _____

Date of independence _____ From _____

Chief of state _____

Head of government _____

Name for citizen (e.g., Canadian) _____

Current population _____ World rank in population _____

Life expectancy _____ men _____ women Literacy _____ % male _____ % female

Ethnic groups _____

Major religions _____

Major languages _____

Land area _____ Water area _____ World rank in area _____

Five largest cities and their populations _____

_____

Bordering nations _____

_____

Climate _____

Terrain _____

Highest point and its elevation _____

Lowest point and its elevation _____

GDP _____ Per capita GDP _____ World rank in GDP _____

Major natural resources _____

Major industries _____

Chief agricultural products _____

Major exports _____

Major imports _____

Malawi

Gather these facts about Malawi, filling in the blanks.

Capital _____ Type of government _____

Date of independence _____ From _____

Chief of state _____ _____

Head of government _____

Name for citizen (e.g., Canadian) _____

Current population _____ World rank in population _____

Life expectancy _____ men _____ women   Literacy _____ % male _____ % female

Ethnic groups _____

Major religions _____

Major languages _____

Land area _____ Water area _____ World rank in area _____

Five largest cities and their populations _____

_____

Bordering nations _____

_____

Climate _____

Terrain _____

Highest point and its elevation _____

Lowest point and its elevation _____

GDP _____ Per capita GDP _____ World rank in GDP _____

Major natural resources _____

Major industries _____

Chief agricultural products _____

Major exports _____

Major imports _____

Mauritius

Gather these facts about Mauritius, filling in the blanks.

Capital _____ _____ Type of government _____

Date of independence _____ From _____

Chief of state _____

Head of government _____

Name for citizen (e.g., Canadian) _____

Current population _____ World rank in population _____

Life expectancy _____ men _____ women Literacy _____ % male _____ % female

Ethnic groups _____

Major religions _____

Major languages _____

Land area _____ Water area _____ World rank in area _____

Five largest cities and their populations _____

_____

Bordering nations _____

_____

Climate _____

Terrain _____

Highest point and its elevation _____

Lowest point and its elevation _____

GDP _____ Per capita GDP _____ World rank in GDP _____

Major natural resources _____

Major industries _____

Chief agricultural products _____

Major exports _____

Major imports _____

Mozambique

Gather these facts about Mozambique, filling in the blanks.

Capital _____ Type of government _____

Date of independence _____ From _____

Chief of state _____ _____

Head of government _____

Name for citizen (e.g., Canadian) _____

Current population _____ World rank in population _____

Life expectancy _____ men _____ women Literacy _____ % male _____ % female

Ethnic groups _____

Major religions _____

Major languages _____

Land area _____ Water area _____ World rank in area _____

Five largest cities and their populations _____

_____

Bordering nations _____

_____

Climate _____

Terrain _____

Highest point and its elevation _____

Lowest point and its elevation _____

GDP _____ Per capita GDP _____ World rank in GDP _____

Major natural resources _____

Major industries _____

Chief agricultural products _____

Major exports _____

Major imports _____

Namibia

Gather these facts about Namibia, filling in the blanks.

Capital _____ _____ Type of government _____

Date of independence _____ From _____ _____

Chief of state _____

Head of government _____

Name for citizen (e.g., Canadian) _____

Current population _____ World rank in population _____

Life expectancy _____ men _____ women Literacy _____ % male _____ % female

Ethnic groups _____

Major religions _____

Major languages _____

Land area _____ Water area _____ World rank in area _____

Five largest cities and their populations _____

_____

Bordering nations _____

_____

Climate _____

Terrain _____

Highest point and its elevation _____

Lowest point and its elevation _____

GDP _____ Per capita GDP _____ World rank in GDP _____

Major natural resources _____

Major industries _____

Chief agricultural products _____

Major exports _____

Major imports _____

Seychelles

Gather these facts about Seychelles, filling in the blanks.

Capital _____ Type of government _____

Date of independence _____ From _____

Chief of state _____

Head of government _____

Name for citizen (e.g., Canadian) _____

Current population _____ World rank in population _____

Life expectancy _____ men _____ women Literacy _____ % male _____ % female

Ethnic groups _____

Major religions _____

Major languages _____

Land area _____ Water area _____ World rank in area _____

Five largest cities and their populations _____

_____

Bordering nations _____

_____

Climate _____

Terrain _____

Highest point and its elevation _____

Lowest point and its elevation _____

GDP _____ Per capita GDP _____ World rank in GDP _____

Major natural resources _____

Major industries _____

Chief agricultural products _____

Major exports _____

Major imports _____

145

South Africa

Gather these facts about South Africa, filling in the blanks.

Capital _____ _____ Type of government _____

Date of independence _____ From _____

Chief of state _____

Head of government _____

Name for citizen (e.g., Canadian) _____

Current population _____ World rank in population _____

Life expectancy _____ men _____ women Literacy _____ % male _____ % female

Ethnic groups _____

Major religions _____

Major languages _____

Land area _____ Water area _____ World rank in area _____

Five largest cities and their populations _____

_____

Bordering nations _____

_____

Climate _____

Terrain _____

Highest point and its elevation _____

Lowest point and its elevation _____

GDP _____ Per capita GDP _____ World rank in GDP _____

Major natural resources _____

Major industries _____

Chief agricultural products _____

Major exports _____

Major imports _____

Swaziland

Gather these facts about Swaziland, filling in the blanks.

Capital _____ Type of government _____

Date of independence _____ From _____

Chief of state _____ _____

Head of government _____

Name for citizen (e.g., Canadian) _____

Current population _____ World rank in population _____

Life expectancy _____ men _____ women   Literacy _____ % male _____ % female

Ethnic groups _____

Major religions _____

Major languages _____

Land area _____ Water area _____ World rank in area _____

Five largest cities and their populations _____

_____

Bordering nations _____

_____

Climate _____

Terrain _____

Highest point and its elevation _____

Lowest point and its elevation _____

GDP _____ Per capita GDP _____ World rank in GDP _____

Major natural resources _____

Major industries _____

Chief agricultural products _____

Major exports _____

Major imports _____

Zambia

Gather these facts about Zambia, filling in the blanks.

Capital _____ _____ Type of government _____

Date of independence _____ From _____

Chief of state _____

Head of government _____

Name for citizen (e.g., Canadian) _____

Current population _____ World rank in population _____

Life expectancy _____ men _____ women   Literacy _____ % male _____ % female

Ethnic groups _____

Major religions _____

Major languages _____

Land area _____ Water area _____ World rank in area _____

Five largest cities and their populations _____

_____

Bordering nations _____

_____

Climate _____

Terrain _____

Highest point and its elevation _____

Lowest point and its elevation _____

GDP _____ Per capita GDP _____ World rank in GDP _____

Major natural resources _____

Major industries _____

Chief agricultural products _____

Major exports _____

Major imports _____

Zimbabwe

Gather these facts about Zimbabwe, filling in the blanks.

Capital _____ Type of government _____

Date of independence _____ From _____

Chief of state _____ _____

Head of government _____

Name for citizen (e.g., Canadian) _____

Current population _____ World rank in population _____

Life expectancy _____ men _____ women Literacy _____ % male _____ % female

Ethnic groups _____

Major religions _____

Major languages _____

Land area _____ Water area _____ World rank in area _____

Five largest cities and their populations _____

_____

Bordering nations _____

_____

Climate _____

Terrain _____

Highest point and its elevation _____

Lowest point and its elevation _____

GDP _____ Per capita GDP _____ World rank in GDP _____

Major natural resources _____

Major industries _____

Chief agricultural products _____

Major exports _____

Major imports _____

Europe

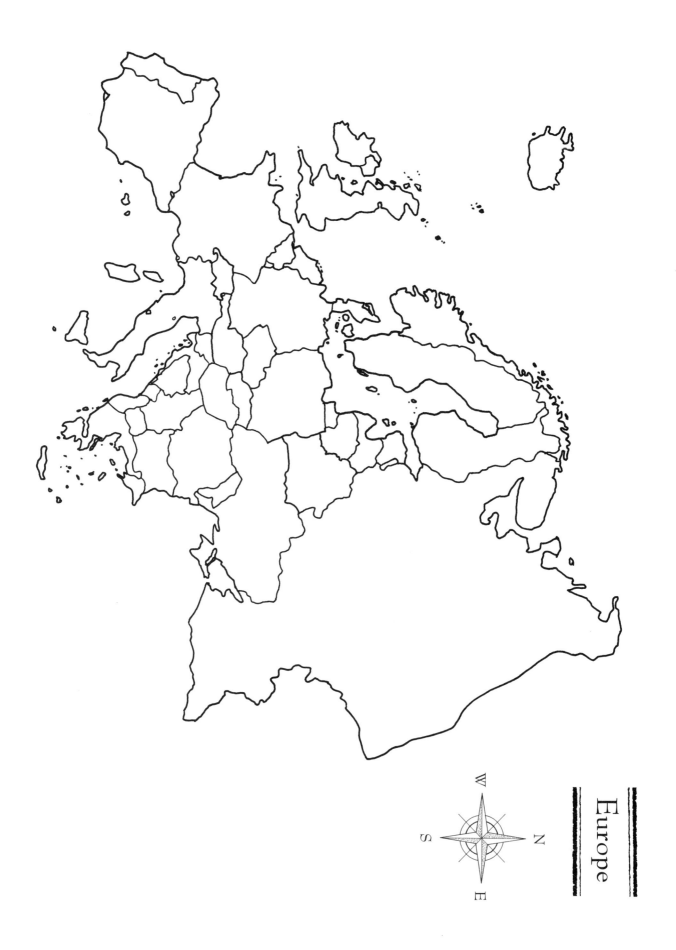

Europe

Europe

Gather these facts about the continent of Europe, filling in the blanks.

Total land area _____ Rank in area _____ of 7

Total population _____ Rank in population _____ of 7

Major languages _____

Major religions _____

Major natural resources _____

Longest river _____

Highest mountain _____

Lowest point _____

Largest lake _____

Biggest desert _____

Biggest island _____

Three largest cities _____

Number of independent countries _____

Largest country _____

Smallest country _____

Most populous country _____

Least populous country _____

Most densely populated country _____

Least densely populated country _____

Largest dependent territory _____

Smallest dependent territory _____

Most populous dependent territory _____

Map It!

On the political map of Europe, label each independent country and its capital. Then use colored pencils to make each country a different color than the countries that border it.

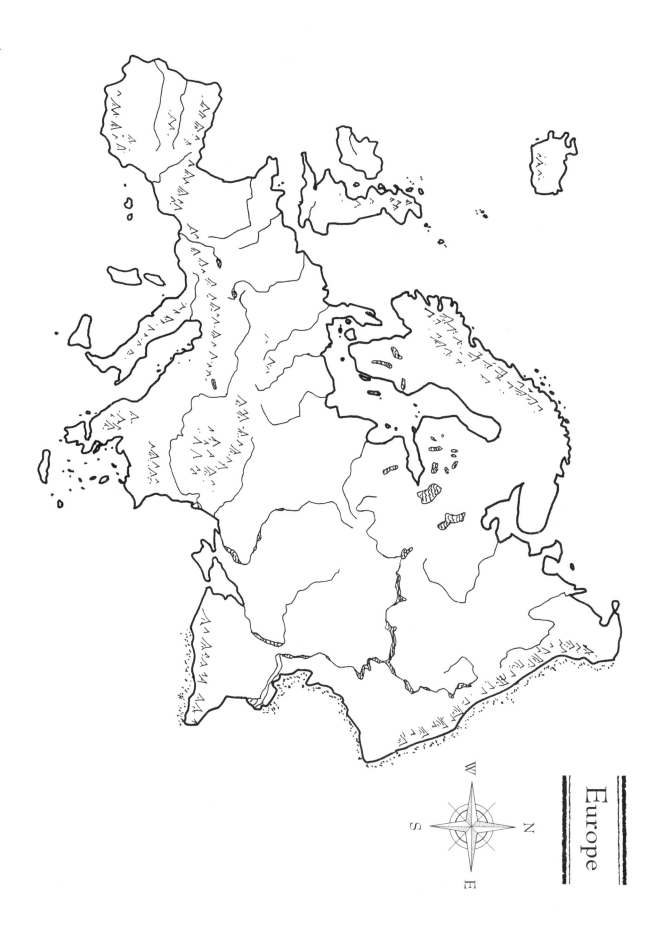

Europe

Map It!

Use this worksheet to organize your information as you research the following geographical features of Europe. This will help you be aware of the locations of all the items you will map before you actually begin so that you can use the space well. Finally, mark each item on the physical map of the continent.

Europe's major landforms (e.g., mountain ranges, plains, plateaus) _____
_____
_____
_____

Europe's major rivers and river basins _____
_____
_____
_____

Europe's major inland bodies of water _____
_____
_____

Europe's deserts _____
_____
_____

Europe's major islands, peninsulas, and capes _____
_____
_____

Bodies of water that border Europe _____
_____
_____

Europe's highest and lowest points and their elevations _____
_____

Any of the following lines of latitude that intersect Europe: Arctic Circle, Tropic of Cancer, Equator, Tropic of Capricorn, Antarctic Circle _____
_____

Any other special geographical features _____
_____
_____

Nordic Europe

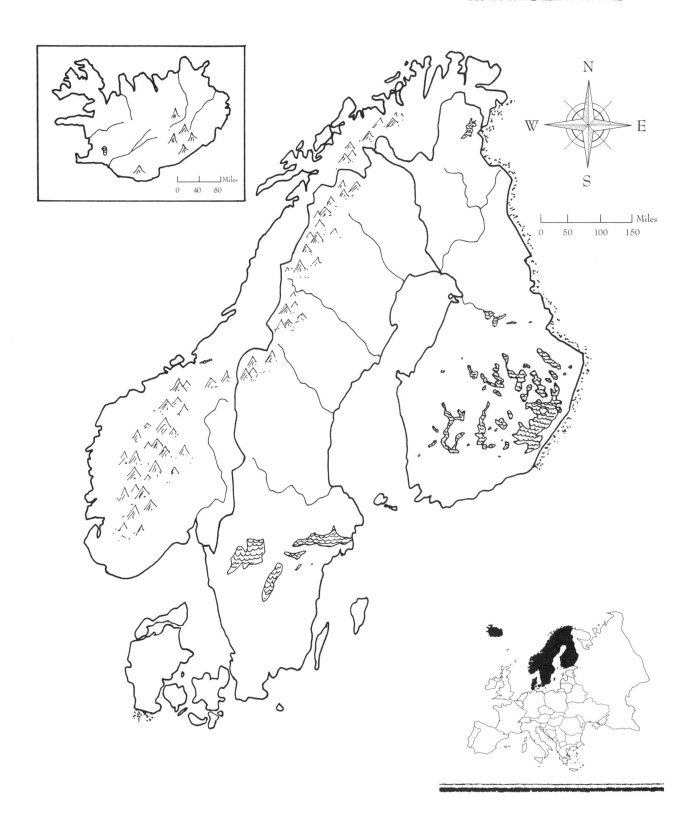

Map It!

Use this worksheet to organize your information as you research the following geographical features of Nordic Europe. This will help you be aware of the locations of all the items you will map before you actually begin so that you can use the space well. If the region doesn't have one of the features listed, simply write "none" on the blank line. Finally, mark each item on the map of the region.

The name of each independent country and its capital city _____

_____

_____

_____

Five other important cities in the region _____

_____

The region's major landforms (e.g., mountain ranges, plains, plateaus) _____

_____

_____

_____

The region's major rivers and river basins _____

_____

_____

_____

The region's major inland bodies of water _____

_____

_____

The region's deserts _____

_____

The region's important islands, peninsulas, and capes _____

_____

_____

Bodies of water that border the region _____

_____

_____

Any other special geographical features _____

_____

Denmark

Gather these facts about Denmark, filling in the blanks.

Capital _____ Type of government _____

Date of independence _____ From _____

Chief of state _____

Head of government _____

Name for citizen (e.g., Canadian) _____

Current population _____ World rank in population _____

Life expectancy _____ men _____ women Literacy _____ % male _____ % female

Ethnic groups _____

Major religions _____

Major languages _____

Land area _____ Water area _____ World rank in area _____

Five largest cities and their populations _____

_____

Bordering nations _____

_____

Climate _____

Terrain _____

Highest point and its elevation _____

Lowest point and its elevation _____

GDP _____ Per capita GDP _____ World rank in GDP _____

Major natural resources _____

Major industries _____

Chief agricultural products _____

Major exports _____

Major imports _____

Finland

Gather these facts about Finland, filling in the blanks.

Capital _____ Type of government _____

Date of independence _____ From _____

Chief of state _____ _____

Head of government _____

Name for citizen (e.g., Canadian) _____

Current population _____ World rank in population _____

Life expectancy _____ men _____ women   Literacy _____ % male _____ % female

Ethnic groups _____

Major religions _____

Major languages _____

Land area _____ Water area _____ World rank in area _____

Five largest cities and their populations _____

_____

Bordering nations _____

_____

Climate _____

Terrain _____

Highest point and its elevation _____ _____

Lowest point and its elevation _____

GDP _____ Per capita GDP _____ World rank in GDP _____

Major natural resources _____

Major industries _____

Chief agricultural products _____

Major exports _____

Major imports _____

Iceland

Gather these facts about Iceland, filling in the blanks.

Capital _____ _____ Type of government _____

Date of independence _____ From _____

Chief of state _____

Head of government _____

Name for citizen (e.g., Canadian) _____

Current population _____ World rank in population _____

Life expectancy_____ men _____ women   Literacy_____ % male _____ % female

Ethnic groups _____

Major religions _____

Major languages _____

Land area _____ Water area _____ World rank in area _____

Five largest cities and their populations _____

_____

Bordering nations _____

_____

Climate _____

Terrain _____

Highest point and its elevation _____

Lowest point and its elevation _____

GDP_____ Per capita GDP _____ World rank in GDP _____

Major natural resources _____

Major industries _____

Chief agricultural products _____

Major exports _____

Major imports _____

Norway

Gather these facts about Norway, filling in the blanks.

Capital _____ Type of government _____

Date of independence _____ From _____

Chief of state _____ _____

Head of government _____

Name for citizen (e.g., Canadian) _____

Current population _____ World rank in population _____

Life expectancy _____ men _____ women Literacy _____ % male _____ % female

Ethnic groups _____

Major religions _____

Major languages _____

Land area _____ Water area _____ World rank in area _____

Five largest cities and their populations _____

_____

Bordering nations _____

_____

Climate _____

Terrain _____

Highest point and its elevation _____ _____

Lowest point and its elevation _____

GDP _____ Per capita GDP _____ World rank in GDP _____

Major natural resources _____

Major industries _____

Chief agricultural products _____

Major exports _____

Major imports _____

Sweden

Gather these facts about Sweden, filling in the blanks.

Capital _____ _____ Type of government _____

Date of independence _____ From _____

Chief of state _____

Head of government _____

Name for citizen (e.g., Canadian) _____

Current population _____ World rank in population _____

Life expectancy _____ men _____ women   Literacy _____ % male _____ % female

Ethnic groups _____

Major religions _____

Major languages _____

Land area _____ Water area _____ World rank in area _____

Five largest cities and their populations _____

_____

Bordering nations _____

_____

Climate _____

Terrain _____

Highest point and its elevation _____

Lowest point and its elevation _____

GDP_____ Per capita GDP _____ World rank in GDP _____

Major natural resources _____

Major industries _____

Chief agricultural products _____

Major exports _____

Major imports _____

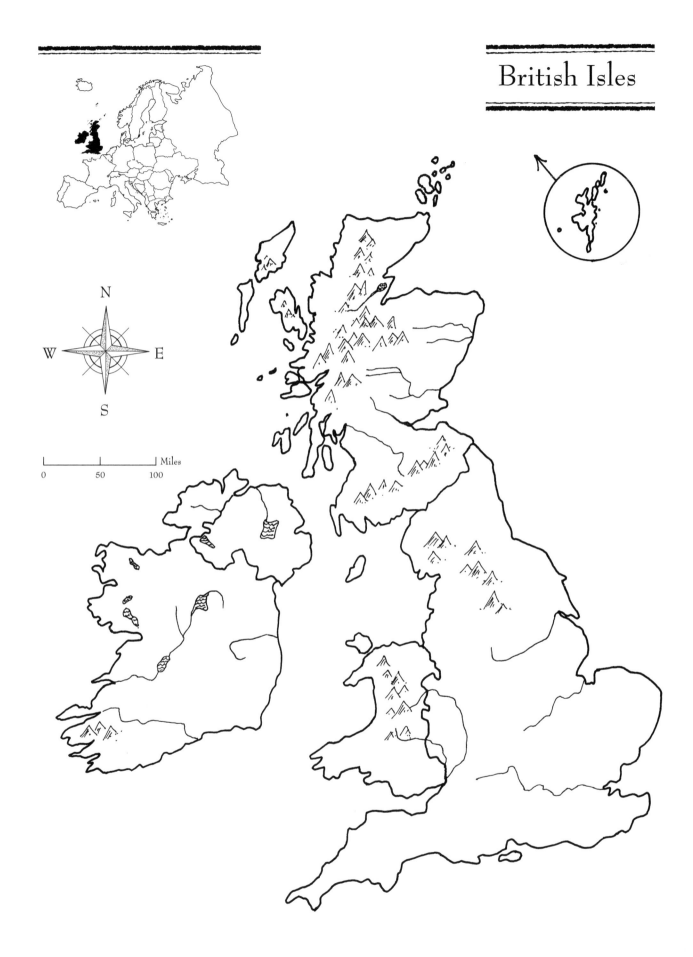

British Isles

N
W E
S

Miles
0   50   100

Map It!

Use this worksheet to organize your information as you research the following geographical features of the British Isles. This will help you be aware of the locations of all the items you will map before you actually begin so that you can use the space well. If the region doesn't have one of the features listed, simply write "none" on the blank line. Finally, mark each item on the map of the region.

The name of each independent country and its capital city _____

_____

_____

_____

Five other important cities in the region _____

_____

The region's major landforms (e.g., mountain ranges, plains, plateaus) _____

_____

_____

_____

The region's major rivers and river basins _____

_____

_____

_____

The region's major inland bodies of water _____

_____

_____

The region's deserts _____

_____

The region's important islands, peninsulas, and capes _____

_____

_____

Bodies of water that border the region _____

_____

_____

Any other special geographical features _____

_____

Ireland

Gather these facts about Ireland, filling in the blanks.

Capital _____ Type of government _____

Date of independence _____ From _____

Chief of state _____

Head of government _____

Name for citizen (e.g., Canadian) _____

Current population _____ World rank in population _____

Life expectancy _____ men _____ women   Literacy _____ % male _____ % female

Ethnic groups _____

Major religions _____

Major languages _____

Land area _____ Water area _____ World rank in area _____

Five largest cities and their populations _____

_____

Bordering nations _____

_____

Climate _____

Terrain _____

Highest point and its elevation _____

Lowest point and its elevation _____

GDP _____ Per capita GDP _____ World rank in GDP _____

Major natural resources _____

Major industries _____

Chief agricultural products _____

Major exports _____

Major imports _____

United Kingdom

Gather these facts about the United Kingdom, filling in the blanks.

Capital _____ Type of government _____

Date of independence _____ From _____

Chief of state _____

Head of government _____

Name for citizen (e.g., Canadian) _____

Current population _____ World rank in population _____

Life expectancy _____ men _____ women Literacy _____ % male _____ % female

Ethnic groups _____

Major religions _____

Major languages _____

Land area _____ Water area _____ World rank in area _____

Five largest cities and their populations _____

_____

Bordering nations _____

_____

Climate _____

Terrain _____

Highest point and its elevation _____

Lowest point and its elevation _____

GDP _____ Per capita GDP _____ World rank in GDP _____

Major natural resources _____

Major industries _____

Chief agricultural products _____

Major exports _____

Major imports _____

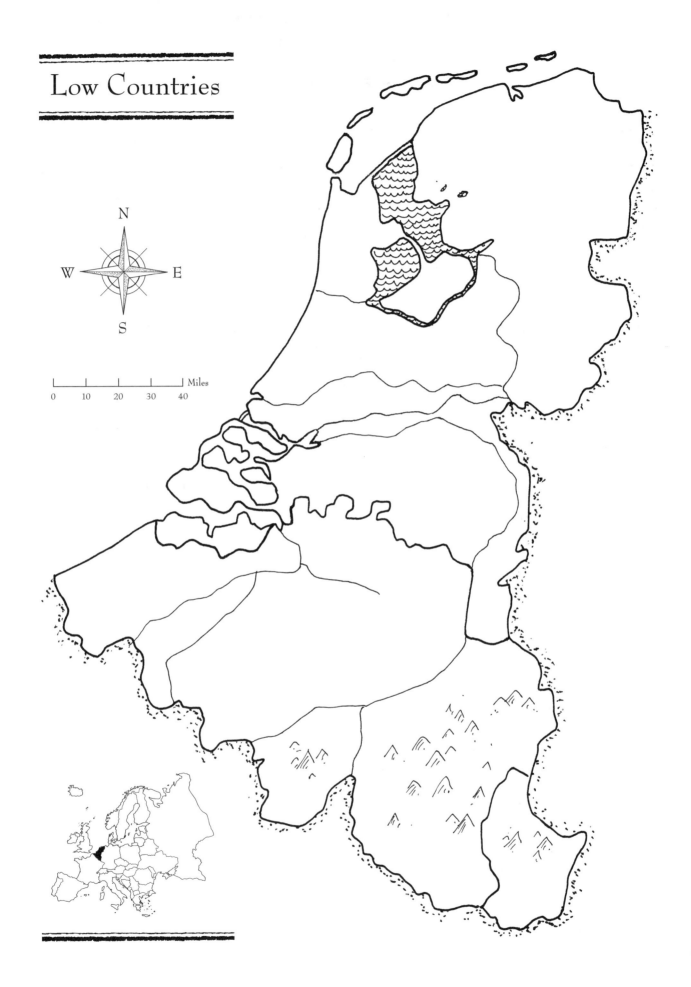

Map It!

Use this worksheet to organize your information as you research the following geographical features of the Low Countries. This will help you be aware of the locations of all the items you will map before you actually begin so that you can use the space well. If the region doesn't have one of the features listed, simply write "none" on the blank line. Finally, mark each item on the map of the region.

The name of each independent country and its capital city _____

_____

_____

_____

Five other important cities in the region _____

_____

The region's major landforms (e.g., mountain ranges, plains, plateaus) _____

_____

_____

_____

The region's major rivers and river basins _____

_____

_____

_____

The region's major inland bodies of water _____

_____

_____

The region's deserts _____

_____

The region's important islands, peninsulas, and capes _____

_____

_____

Bodies of water that border the region _____

_____

_____

Any other special geographical features _____

_____

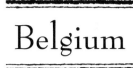

Belgium

Gather these facts about Belgium, filling in the blanks.

Capital _____ Type of government _____

Date of independence _____ From _____

Chief of state _____

Head of government _____

Name for citizen (e.g., Canadian) _____

Current population _____ World rank in population _____

Life expectancy _____ men _____ women   Literacy _____ % male _____ % female

Ethnic groups _____

Major religions _____

Major languages _____

Land area _____ Water area _____ World rank in area _____

Five largest cities and their populations _____

_____

Bordering nations _____

_____

Climate _____

Terrain _____

Highest point and its elevation _____

Lowest point and its elevation _____

GDP _____ Per capita GDP _____ World rank in GDP _____

Major natural resources _____

Major industries _____

Chief agricultural products _____

Major exports _____

Major imports _____

Luxembourg

Gather these facts about Luxembourg, filling in the blanks.

Capital _____ Type of government _____

Date of independence _____ From _____

Chief of state _____

Head of government _____

Name for citizen (e.g., Canadian) _____

Current population _____ World rank in population _____

Life expectancy _____ men _____ women Literacy _____ % male _____ % female

Ethnic groups _____

Major religions _____

Major languages _____

Land area _____ Water area _____ World rank in area _____

Five largest cities and their populations _____

_____

Bordering nations _____

_____

Climate _____

Terrain _____

Highest point and its elevation _____

Lowest point and its elevation _____

GDP _____ Per capita GDP _____ World rank in GDP _____

Major natural resources _____

Major industries _____

Chief agricultural products _____

Major exports _____

Major imports _____

Netherlands

Gather these facts about the Netherlands, filling in the blanks.

Capital _____ Type of government _____

Date of independence _____ From _____

Chief of state _____

Head of government _____

Name for citizen (e.g., Canadian) _____

Current population _____ World rank in population _____

Life expectancy _____ men _____ women Literacy _____ % male _____ % female

Ethnic groups _____

Major religions _____

Major languages _____

Land area _____ Water area _____ World rank in area _____

Five largest cities and their populations _____

_____

Bordering nations _____

_____

Climate _____

Terrain _____

Highest point and its elevation _____

Lowest point and its elevation _____

GDP_____ Per capita GDP _____ World rank in GDP _____

Major natural resources _____

Major industries _____

Chief agricultural products _____

Major exports _____

Major imports _____

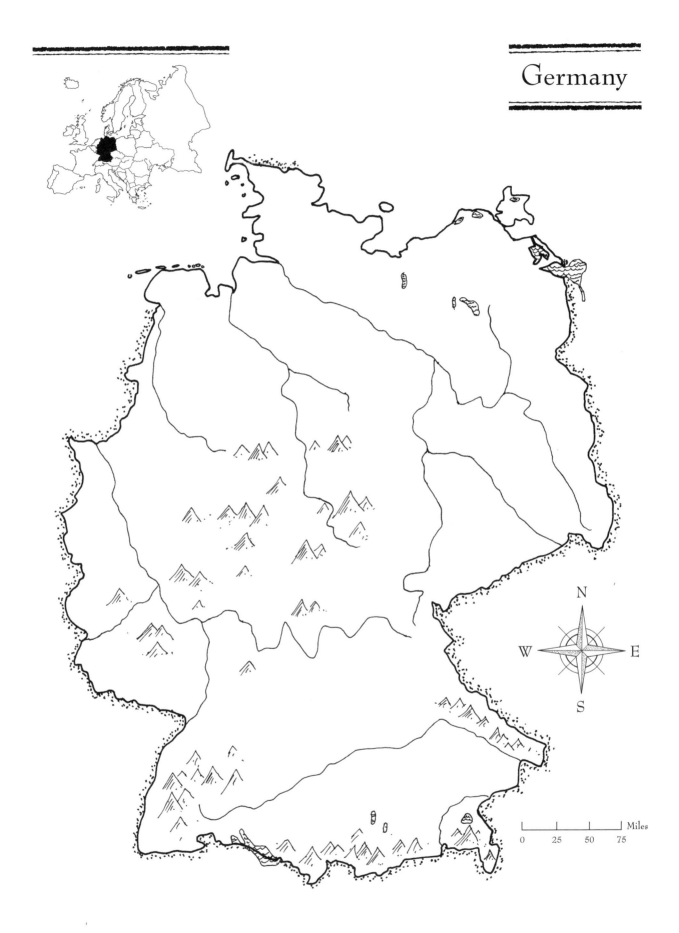

Germany

Map It!

Use this worksheet to organize your information as you research the following geographical features of Germany. This will help you be aware of the locations of all the items you will map before you actually begin so that you can use the space well. If Germany doesn't have one of the features listed, simply write "none" on the blank line. Finally, mark each item on the map of the country.

Germany's capital city   _____   _____

Germany's five largest cities   _____

_____

Germany's major landforms (e.g., mountain ranges, plains, plateaus)   _____

_____

_____

_____

Germany's highest and lowest points and their elevations   _____

_____

Germany's major rivers and river basins   _____

_____

_____

Germany's major inland bodies of water   _____

_____

_____

Germany's deserts   _____

_____

Germany's important islands, peninsulas, and capes   _____

_____

_____

Bodies of water that border Germany   _____

_____

_____

Any other special geographical features   _____

_____

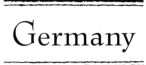

Germany

Gather these facts about Germany, filling in the blanks.

Capital _____ Type of government _____

Date of independence _____ From _____

Chief of state _____

Head of government _____

Name for citizen (e.g., Canadian) _____

Current population _____ World rank in population _____

Life expectancy _____ men _____ women Literacy _____ % male _____ % female

Ethnic groups _____

Major religions _____

Major languages _____

Land area _____ Water area _____ World rank in area _____

Five largest cities and their populations _____

_____

Bordering nations _____

_____

Climate _____

Terrain _____

Highest point and its elevation _____

Lowest point and its elevation _____

GDP _____ Per capita GDP _____ World rank in GDP _____

Major natural resources _____

Major industries _____

Chief agricultural products _____

Major exports _____

Major imports _____

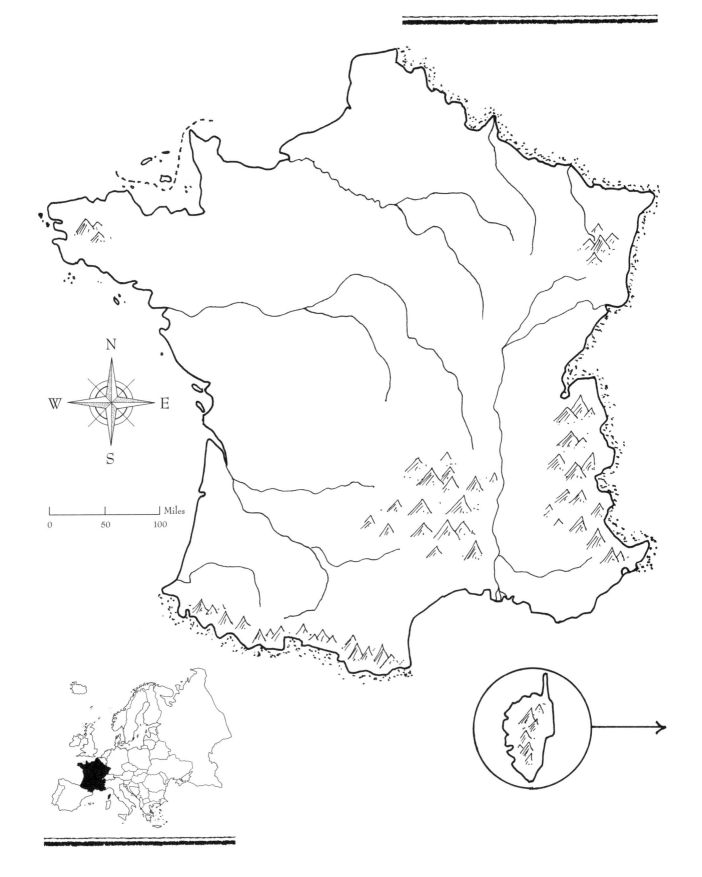

Map It!

Use this worksheet to organize your information as you research the following geographical features of France and Monaco. This will help you be aware of the locations of all the items you will map before you actually begin so that you can use the space well. If the region doesn't have one of the features listed, simply write "none" on the blank line. Finally, mark each item on the map of the region.

The name of each independent country and its capital city _____

_____

_____

_____

France's five largest cities _____

_____

France's major landforms (e.g., mountain ranges, plains, plateaus) _____

_____

_____

_____

France's major rivers and river basins _____

_____

_____

_____

France's major inland bodies of water _____

_____

_____

France's deserts _____

_____

France's important islands, peninsulas, and capes _____

_____

_____

Bodies of water that border France _____

_____

_____

Any other special geographical features _____

_____

France

Gather these facts about France, filling in the blanks.

Capital _____ Type of government _____

Date of independence _____ From _____

Chief of state _____

Head of government _____

Name for citizen (e.g., Canadian) _____

Current population _____ World rank in population _____

Life expectancy _____ men _____ women Literacy _____ % male _____ % female

Ethnic groups _____

Major religions _____

Major languages _____

Land area _____ Water area _____ World rank in area _____

Five largest cities and their populations _____

_____

Bordering nations _____

_____

Climate _____

Terrain _____

Highest point and its elevation _____

Lowest point and its elevation _____

GDP _____ Per capita GDP _____ World rank in GDP _____

Major natural resources _____

Major industries _____

Chief agricultural products _____

Major exports _____

Major imports _____

Monaco

Gather these facts about Monaco, filling in the blanks.

Capital _____ Type of government _____

Date of independence _____ From _____

Chief of state _____

Head of government _____

Name for citizen (e.g., Canadian) _____

Current population _____ World rank in population _____

Life expectancy _____ men _____ women Literacy _____ % male _____ % female

Ethnic groups _____

Major religions _____

Major languages _____

Land area _____ Water area _____ World rank in area _____

Five largest cities and their populations _____

_____

Bordering nations _____

_____

Climate _____

Terrain _____

Highest point and its elevation _____

Lowest point and its elevation _____

GDP _____ Per capita GDP _____ World rank in GDP _____

Major natural resources _____

Major industries _____

Chief agricultural products _____

Major exports _____

Major imports _____

Iberian Peninsula

0
25
50
75
100
Miles

W
S   N
E

Map It!

Use this worksheet to organize your information as you research the following geographical features of the Iberian Peninsula. This will help you be aware of the locations of all the items you will map before you actually begin so that you can use the space well. If the region doesn't have one of the features listed, simply write "none" on the blank line. Finally, mark each item on the map of the region.

The name of each independent country and its capital city _____
_____
_____
_____

Five other important cities in the region _____
_____

The region's major landforms (e.g., mountain ranges, plains, plateaus) _____
_____
_____
_____

The region's major rivers and river basins _____
_____
_____
_____

The region's major inland bodies of water _____
_____
_____

The region's deserts _____
_____

The region's important islands, peninsulas, and capes _____
_____
_____

Bodies of water that border the region _____
_____
_____

Any other special geographical features _____
_____

Andorra

Gather these facts about Andorra, filling in the blanks.

Capital _____ Type of government _____ _____

Date of independence _____ From _____

Chief of state _____

Head of government _____

Name for citizen (e.g., Canadian) _____

Current population _____ World rank in population _____

Life expectancy _____ men _____ women   Literacy _____ % male _____ % female

Ethnic groups _____

Major religions _____

Major languages _____

Land area _____ Water area _____ World rank in area _____

Five largest cities and their populations _____

_____

Bordering nations _____

_____

Climate _____

Terrain _____

Highest point and its elevation _____

Lowest point and its elevation _____

GDP_____ Per capita GDP _____ World rank in GDP _____

Major natural resources _____

Major industries _____

Chief agricultural products _____

Major exports _____

Major imports _____

Portugal

Gather these facts about Portugal, filling in the blanks.

Capital _____ Type of government _____

Date of independence _____ From _____

Chief of state _____

Head of government _____

Name for citizen (e.g., Canadian) _____

Current population _____ World rank in population _____

Life expectancy _____ men _____ women   Literacy _____ % male _____ % female

Ethnic groups _____

Major religions _____

Major languages _____

Land area _____ Water area _____ World rank in area _____

Five largest cities and their populations _____

_____

Bordering nations _____

_____

Climate _____

Terrain _____

Highest point and its elevation _____

Lowest point and its elevation _____

GDP_____ Per capita GDP _____ World rank in GDP _____

Major natural resources _____

Major industries _____

Chief agricultural products _____

Major exports _____

Major imports _____

Spain

Gather these facts about Spain, filling in the blanks.

Capital _____ Type of government _____ _____

Date of independence _____ From _____

Chief of state _____

Head of government _____

Name for citizen (e.g., Canadian) _____

Current population _____ World rank in population _____

Life expectancy _____ men _____ women   Literacy _____ % male _____ % female

Ethnic groups _____

Major religions _____

Major languages _____

Land area _____ Water area _____ World rank in area _____

Five largest cities and their populations _____

_____

Bordering nations _____

_____

Climate _____

Terrain _____

Highest point and its elevation _____

Lowest point and its elevation _____

GDP _____ Per capita GDP _____ World rank in GDP _____

Major natural resources _____

Major industries _____

Chief agricultural products _____

Major exports _____

Major imports _____

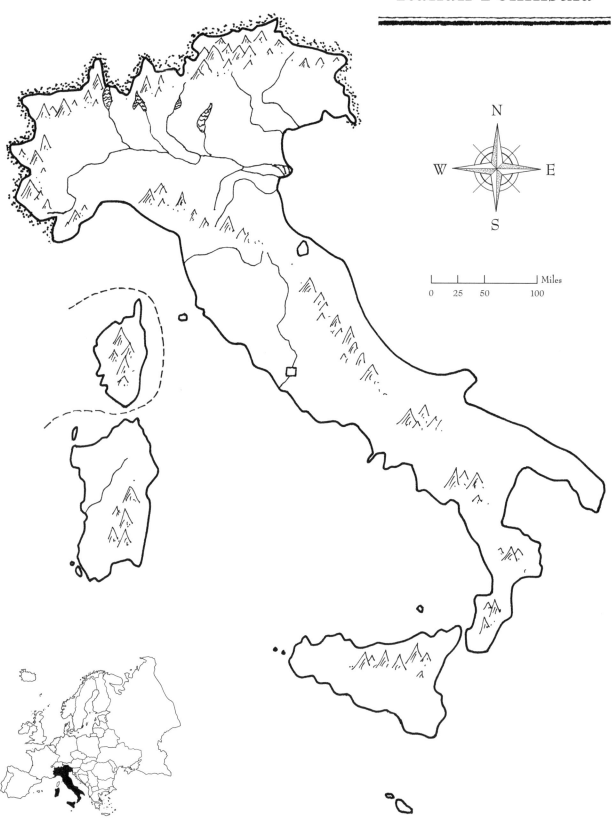

Italian Peninsula

Map It!

Use this worksheet to organize your information as you research the following geographical features of the Italian Peninsula. This will help you be aware of the locations of all the items you will map before you actually begin so that you can use the space well. If the region doesn't have one of the features listed, simply write "none" on the blank line. Finally, mark each item on the map of the region.

The name of each independent country and its capital city _____

_____

_____

_____

Five other important cities in the region _____

_____

The region's major landforms (e.g., mountain ranges, plains, plateaus) _____

_____

_____

_____

The region's major rivers and river basins _____

_____

_____

_____

The region's major inland bodies of water _____

_____

_____

The region's deserts _____

_____

The region's important islands, peninsulas, and capes _____

_____

_____

Bodies of water that border the region _____

_____

_____

Any other special geographical features _____

_____

Italy

Gather these facts about Italy, filling in the blanks.

Capital _____ Type of government _____

Date of independence _____ From _____

Chief of state _____

Head of government _____

Name for citizen (e.g., Canadian) _____

Current population _____ World rank in population _____

Life expectancy _____ men _____ women Literacy _____ % male _____ % female

Ethnic groups _____

Major religions _____

Major languages _____

Land area _____ Water area _____ World rank in area _____

Five largest cities and their populations _____

_____

Bordering nations _____

_____

Climate _____

Terrain _____

Highest point and its elevation _____

Lowest point and its elevation _____

GDP _____ Per capita GDP _____ World rank in GDP _____

Major natural resources _____

Major industries _____

Chief agricultural products _____

Major exports _____

Major imports _____

Malta

Gather these facts about Malta, filling in the blanks.

Capital _____ Type of government _____

Date of independence _____ From _____

Chief of state _____

Head of government _____

Name for citizen (e.g., Canadian) _____

Current population _____ World rank in population _____

Life expectancy _____ men _____ women Literacy _____ % male _____ % female

Ethnic groups _____

Major religions _____

Major languages _____

Land area _____ Water area _____ World rank in area _____

Five largest cities and their populations _____

_____

Bordering nations _____

_____

Climate _____

Terrain _____

Highest point and its elevation _____

Lowest point and its elevation _____

GDP _____ Per capita GDP _____ World rank in GDP _____

Major natural resources _____

Major industries _____

Chief agricultural products _____

Major exports _____

Major imports _____

San Marino

Gather these facts about San Marino, filling in the blanks.

Capital _____ Type of government _____

Date of independence _____ From _____

Chief of state _____

Head of government _____

Name for citizen (e.g., Canadian) _____

Current population _____ World rank in population _____

Life expectancy _____ men _____ women   Literacy _____ % male _____ % female

Ethnic groups _____

Major religions _____

Major languages _____

Land area _____ Water area _____ World rank in area _____

Five largest cities and their populations _____

_____

Bordering nations _____

_____

Climate _____

Terrain _____

Highest point and its elevation _____

Lowest point and its elevation _____

GDP_____ Per capita GDP _____ World rank in GDP _____

Major natural resources _____

Major industries _____

Chief agricultural products _____

Major exports _____

Major imports _____

Vatican City

Gather these facts about Vatican City, filling in the blanks.

Capital _____ Type of government _____

Date of independence _____ From _____

Chief of state _____

Head of government _____

Name for citizen (e.g., Canadian) _____

Current population _____ World rank in population _____

Life expectancy _____ men _____ women   Literacy _____ % male _____ % female

Ethnic groups _____

Major religions _____

Major languages _____

Land area _____ Water area _____ World rank in area _____

Five largest cities and their populations _____

_____

Bordering nations _____

_____

Climate _____

Terrain _____

Highest point and its elevation _____

Lowest point and its elevation _____

GDP _____ Per capita GDP _____ World rank in GDP _____

Major natural resources _____

Major industries _____

Chief agricultural products _____

Major exports _____

Major imports _____

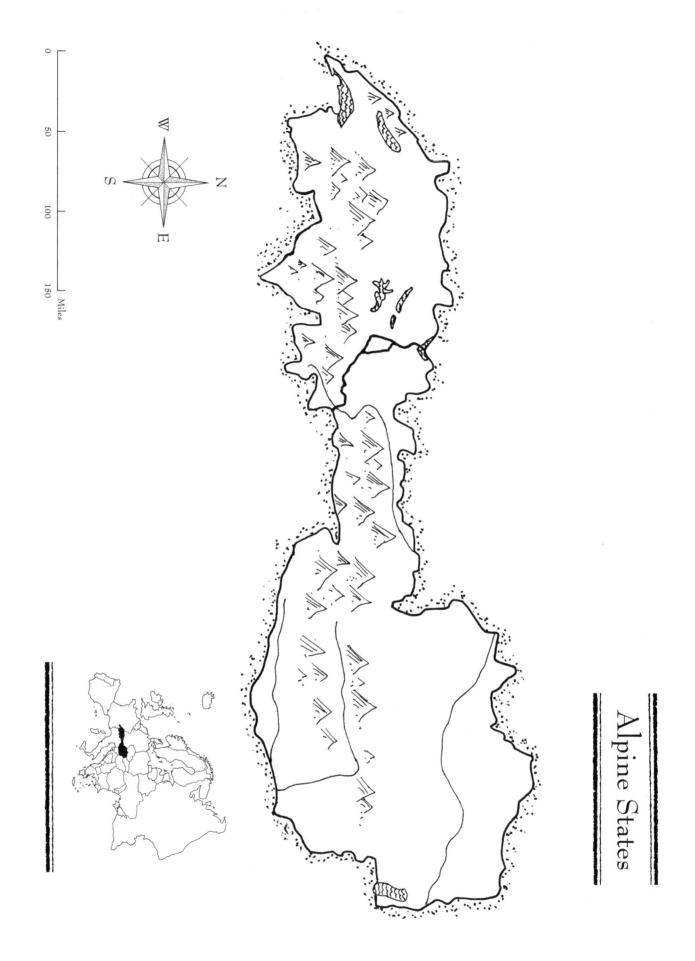

Alpine States

Map It!

Use this worksheet to organize your information as you research the following geographical features of the Alpine States. This will help you be aware of the locations of all the items you will map before you actually begin so that you can use the space well. If the region doesn't have one of the features listed, simply write "none" on the blank line. Finally, mark each item on the map of the region.

The name of each independent country and its capital city _____

_____

_____

_____

Five other important cities in the region _____

_____

The region's major landforms (e.g., mountain ranges, plains, plateaus) _____

_____

_____

_____

The region's major rivers and river basins _____

_____

_____

_____

The region's major inland bodies of water _____

_____

_____

The region's deserts _____

_____

The region's important islands, peninsulas, and capes _____

_____

_____

Bodies of water that border the region _____

_____

_____

Any other special geographical features _____

_____

Austria

Gather these facts about Austria, filling in the blanks.

Capital _____ Type of government _____

Date of independence _____ From _____

Chief of state _____

Head of government _____

Name for citizen (e.g., Canadian) _____

Current population _____ World rank in population _____

Life expectancy _____ men _____ women Literacy _____ % male _____ % female

Ethnic groups _____

Major religions _____

Major languages _____

Land area _____ Water area _____ World rank in area _____

Five largest cities and their populations _____

_____

Bordering nations _____

_____

Climate _____

Terrain _____

Highest point and its elevation _____

Lowest point and its elevation _____

GDP _____ Per capita GDP _____ World rank in GDP _____

Major natural resources _____

Major industries _____

Chief agricultural products _____

Major exports _____

Major imports _____

Liechtenstein

Gather these facts about Liechtenstein, filling in the blanks.

Capital _____ Type of government _____

Date of independence _____ From _____

Chief of state _____

Head of government _____

Name for citizen (e.g., Canadian) _____

Current population _____ World rank in population _____

Life expectancy _____ men _____ women Literacy _____ % male _____ % female

Ethnic groups _____

Major religions _____

Major languages _____

Land area _____ Water area _____ World rank in area _____

Five largest cities and their populations _____

_____

Bordering nations _____

_____

Climate _____

Terrain _____

Highest point and its elevation _____

Lowest point and its elevation _____

GDP _____ Per capita GDP _____ World rank in GDP _____

Major natural resources _____

Major industries _____

Chief agricultural products _____

Major exports _____

Major imports _____

Switzerland

Gather these facts about Switzerland, filling in the blanks.

Capital _____ Type of government _____

Date of independence _____ From _____

Chief of state _____

Head of government _____

Name for citizen (e.g., Canadian) _____

Current population _____ World rank in population _____

Life expectancy _____ men _____ women Literacy _____ % male _____ % female

Ethnic groups _____

Major religions _____

Major languages _____

Land area _____ Water area _____ World rank in area _____

Five largest cities and their populations _____

_____

Bordering nations _____

_____

Climate _____

Terrain _____

Highest point and its elevation _____

Lowest point and its elevation _____

GDP _____ Per capita GDP _____ World rank in GDP _____

Major natural resources _____

Major industries _____

Chief agricultural products _____

Major exports _____

Major imports _____

Central Europe

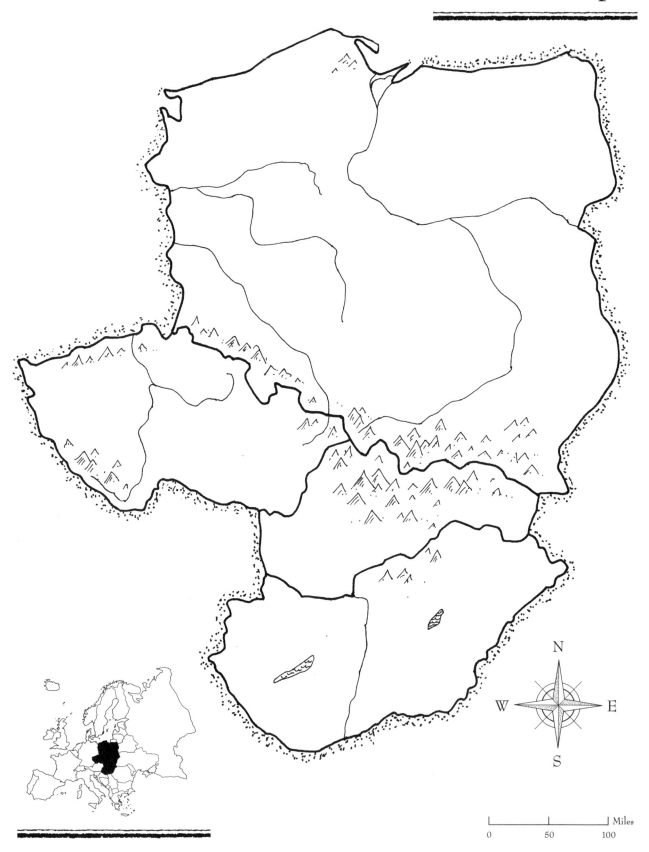

N

W   E

S

		Miles
0	50	100

Map It!

Use this worksheet to organize your information as you research the following geographical features of Central Europe. This will help you be aware of the locations of all the items you will map before you actually begin so that you can use the space well. If the region doesn't have one of the features listed, simply write "none" on the blank line. Finally, mark each item on the map of the region.

The name of each independent country and its capital city _____

_____

_____

_____

Five other important cities in the region _____

_____

The region's major landforms (e.g., mountain ranges, plains, plateaus) _____

_____

_____

_____

The region's major rivers and river basins _____

_____

_____

_____

The region's major inland bodies of water _____

_____

_____

The region's deserts _____

_____

The region's important islands, peninsulas, and capes _____

_____

_____

Bodies of water that border the region _____

_____

_____

Any other special geographical features _____

_____

Czech Republic

Gather these facts about the Czech Republic, filling in the blanks.

Capital _____ Type of government _____

Date of independence _____ From _____

Chief of state _____

Head of government _____

Name for citizen (e.g., Canadian) _____

Current population _____ World rank in population _____

Life expectancy _____ men _____ women Literacy _____ % male _____ % female

Ethnic groups _____

Major religions _____

Major languages _____

Land area _____ Water area _____ World rank in area _____

Five largest cities and their populations _____

_____

Bordering nations _____

_____

Climate _____

Terrain _____

Highest point and its elevation _____

Lowest point and its elevation _____

GDP _____ Per capita GDP _____ World rank in GDP _____

Major natural resources _____

Major industries _____

Chief agricultural products _____

Major exports _____

Major imports _____

Hungary

Gather these facts about Hungary, filling in the blanks.

Capital _____ Type of government _____

Date of independence _____ From _____

Chief of state _____

Head of government _____

Name for citizen (e.g., Canadian) _____

Current population _____ World rank in population _____

Life expectancy _____ men _____ women Literacy _____ % male _____ % female

Ethnic groups _____

Major religions _____

Major languages _____

Land area _____ Water area _____ World rank in area _____

Five largest cities and their populations _____

_____

Bordering nations _____

_____

Climate _____

Terrain _____

Highest point and its elevation _____

Lowest point and its elevation _____

GDP _____ Per capita GDP _____ World rank in GDP _____

Major natural resources _____

Major industries _____

Chief agricultural products _____

Major exports _____

Major imports _____

Poland

Gather these facts about Poland, filling in the blanks.

Capital _____ Type of government _____

Date of independence _____ From _____

Chief of state _____

Head of government _____

Name for citizen (e.g., Canadian) _____

Current population _____ World rank in population _____

Life expectancy _____ men _____ women Literacy _____ % male _____ % female

Ethnic groups _____

Major religions _____

Major languages _____

Land area _____ Water area _____ World rank in area _____

Five largest cities and their populations _____

_____

Bordering nations _____

_____

Climate _____

Terrain _____

Highest point and its elevation _____

Lowest point and its elevation _____

GDP _____ Per capita GDP _____ World rank in GDP _____

Major natural resources _____

Major industries _____

Chief agricultural products _____

Major exports _____

Major imports _____

Slovakia

Gather these facts about Slovakia, filling in the blanks.

Capital _____ Type of government _____

Date of independence _____ From _____

Chief of state _____

Head of government _____

Name for citizen (e.g., Canadian) _____

Current population _____ World rank in population _____

Life expectancy _____ men _____ women Literacy _____ % male _____ % female

Ethnic groups _____

Major religions _____

Major languages _____

Land area _____ Water area _____ World rank in area _____

Five largest cities and their populations _____

_____

Bordering nations _____

_____

Climate _____

Terrain _____

Highest point and its elevation _____

Lowest point and its elevation _____

GDP _____ Per capita GDP _____ World rank in GDP _____

Major natural resources _____

Major industries _____

Chief agricultural products _____

Major exports _____

Major imports _____

Balkan States

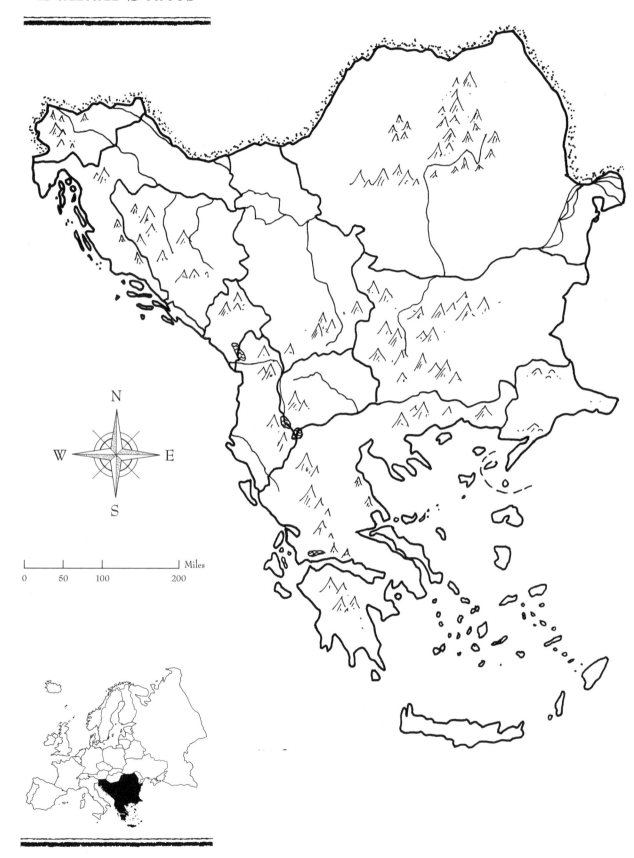

Map It!

Use this worksheet to organize your information as you research the following geographical features of the Balkan States. This will help you be aware of the locations of all the items you will map before you actually begin so that you can use the space well. If the region doesn't have one of the features listed, simply write "none" on the blank line. Finally, mark each item on the map of the region.

The name of each independent country and its capital city _____

_____

_____

_____

_____

_____

_____

The region's major landforms (e.g., mountain ranges, plains, plateaus) _____

_____

_____

_____

The region's major rivers and river basins _____

_____

_____

_____

The region's major inland bodies of water _____

_____

_____

The region's deserts _____

_____

The region's important islands, peninsulas, and capes _____

_____

_____

Bodies of water that border the region _____

_____

_____

Any other special geographical features _____

_____

Albania

Gather these facts about Albania, filling in the blanks.

Capital _____ Type of government _____

Date of independence _____ From _____

Chief of state _____

Head of government _____

Name for citizen (e.g., Canadian) _____

Current population _____ World rank in population _____

Life expectancy _____ men _____ women Literacy _____ % male _____ % female

Ethnic groups _____

Major religions _____

Major languages _____

Land area _____ Water area _____ World rank in area _____

Five largest cities and their populations _____

_____

Bordering nations _____

_____

Climate _____

Terrain _____

Highest point and its elevation _____

Lowest point and its elevation _____

GDP _____ Per capita GDP _____ World rank in GDP _____

Major natural resources _____

Major industries _____

Chief agricultural products _____

Major exports _____

Major imports _____

Bosnia and Herzegovina

Gather these facts about Bosnia and Herzegovina, filling in the blanks.

Capital _____ Type of government _____

Date of independence _____ From _____

Chief of state _____

Head of government _____

Name for citizen (e.g., Canadian) _____

Current population _____ World rank in population _____

Life expectancy _____ men _____ women Literacy _____ % male _____ % female

Ethnic groups _____

Major religions _____

Major languages _____

Land area _____ Water area _____ World rank in area _____

Five largest cities and their populations _____

_____

Bordering nations _____

_____

Climate _____

Terrain _____

Highest point and its elevation _____

Lowest point and its elevation _____

GDP _____ Per capita GDP _____ World rank in GDP _____

Major natural resources _____

Major industries _____

Chief agricultural products _____

Major exports _____

Major imports _____

Bulgaria

Gather these facts about Bulgaria, filling in the blanks.

Capital _____ Type of government _____

Date of independence _____ From _____

Chief of state _____

Head of government _____

Name for citizen (e.g., Canadian) _____

Current population _____ World rank in population _____

Life expectancy _____ men _____ women   Literacy _____ % male _____ % female

Ethnic groups _____

Major religions _____

Major languages _____

Land area _____ Water area _____ World rank in area _____

Five largest cities and their populations _____

_____

Bordering nations _____

_____

Climate _____

Terrain _____

Highest point and its elevation _____

Lowest point and its elevation _____

GDP _____ Per capita GDP _____ World rank in GDP _____

Major natural resources _____

Major industries _____

Chief agricultural products _____

Major exports _____

Major imports _____

Croatia

Gather these facts about Croatia, filling in the blanks.

Capital _____ Type of government _____

Date of independence _____ From _____

Chief of state _____

Head of government _____

Name for citizen (e.g., Canadian) _____

Current population _____ World rank in population _____

Life expectancy _____ men _____ women Literacy _____ % male _____ % female

Ethnic groups _____

Major religions _____

Major languages _____

Land area _____ Water area _____ World rank in area _____

Five largest cities and their populations _____

_____

Bordering nations _____

_____

Climate _____

Terrain _____

Highest point and its elevation _____

Lowest point and its elevation _____

GDP _____ Per capita GDP _____ World rank in GDP _____

Major natural resources _____

Major industries _____

Chief agricultural products _____

Major exports _____

Major imports _____

Greece

Gather these facts about Greece, filling in the blanks.

Capital _____ Type of government _____

Date of independence _____ From _____

Chief of state _____

Head of government _____

Name for citizen (e.g., Canadian) _____

Current population _____ World rank in population _____

Life expectancy _____ men _____ women Literacy _____ % male _____ % female

Ethnic groups _____

Major religions _____

Major languages _____

Land area _____ Water area _____ World rank in area _____

Five largest cities and their populations _____

_____

Bordering nations _____

_____

Climate _____

Terrain _____

Highest point and its elevation _____

Lowest point and its elevation _____

GDP _____ Per capita GDP _____ World rank in GDP _____

Major natural resources _____

Major industries _____

Chief agricultural products _____

Major exports _____

Major imports _____

Macedonia

Gather these facts about Macedonia, filling in the blanks.

Capital _____ Type of government _____

Date of independence _____ From _____

Chief of state _____

Head of government _____

Name for citizen (e.g., Canadian) _____

Current population _____ World rank in population _____

Life expectancy _____ men _____ women Literacy _____ % male _____ % female

Ethnic groups _____

Major religions _____

Major languages _____

Land area _____ Water area _____ World rank in area _____

Five largest cities and their populations _____

_____

Bordering nations _____

_____

Climate _____

Terrain _____

Highest point and its elevation _____

Lowest point and its elevation _____

GDP _____ Per capita GDP _____ World rank in GDP _____

Major natural resources _____

Major industries _____

Chief agricultural products _____

Major exports _____

Major imports _____

Montenegro

Gather these facts about Montenegro, filling in the blanks.

Capital _____ Type of government _____

Date of independence _____ From _____

Chief of state _____

Head of government _____

Name for citizen (e.g., Canadian) _____

Current population _____ World rank in population _____

Life expectancy _____ men _____ women   Literacy _____ % male _____ % female

Ethnic groups _____

Major religions _____

Major languages _____

Land area _____ Water area _____ World rank in area _____

Five largest cities and their populations _____

_____

Bordering nations _____

_____

Climate _____

Terrain _____

Highest point and its elevation _____

Lowest point and its elevation _____

GDP _____ Per capita GDP _____ World rank in GDP _____

Major natural resources _____

Major industries _____

Chief agricultural products _____

Major exports _____

Major imports _____

Romania

Gather these facts about Romania, filling in the blanks.

Capital _____ Type of government _____

Date of independence _____ From _____

Chief of state _____

Head of government _____

Name for citizen (e.g., Canadian) _____

Current population _____ World rank in population _____

Life expectancy _____ men _____ women Literacy _____ % male _____ % female

Ethnic groups _____

Major religions _____

Major languages _____

Land area _____ Water area _____ World rank in area _____

Five largest cities and their populations _____

_____

Bordering nations _____

_____

Climate _____

Terrain _____

Highest point and its elevation _____

Lowest point and its elevation _____

GDP _____ Per capita GDP _____ World rank in GDP _____

Major natural resources _____

Major industries _____

Chief agricultural products _____

Major exports _____

Major imports _____

Serbia

Gather these facts about Serbia, filling in the blanks.

Capital _____ Type of government _____

Date of independence _____ From _____

Chief of state _____

Head of government _____

Name for citizen (e.g., Canadian) _____

Current population _____ World rank in population _____

Life expectancy _____ men _____ women   Literacy _____ % male _____ % female

Ethnic groups _____

Major religions _____

Major languages _____

Land area _____ Water area _____ World rank in area _____

Five largest cities and their populations _____

_____

Bordering nations _____

_____

Climate _____

Terrain _____

Highest point and its elevation _____

Lowest point and its elevation _____

GDP _____ Per capita GDP _____ World rank in GDP _____

Major natural resources _____

Major industries _____

Chief agricultural products _____

Major exports _____

Major imports _____

Slovenia

Gather these facts about Slovenia, filling in the blanks.

Capital _____ Type of government _____

Date of independence _____ From _____

Chief of state _____

Head of government _____

Name for citizen (e.g., Canadian) _____

Current population _____ World rank in population _____

Life expectancy _____ men _____ women Literacy _____ % male _____ % female

Ethnic groups _____

Major religions _____

Major languages _____

Land area _____ Water area _____ World rank in area _____

Five largest cities and their populations _____

_____

Bordering nations _____

_____

Climate _____

Terrain _____

Highest point and its elevation _____

Lowest point and its elevation _____

GDP _____ Per capita GDP _____ World rank in GDP _____

Major natural resources _____

Major industries _____

Chief agricultural products _____

Major exports _____

Major imports _____

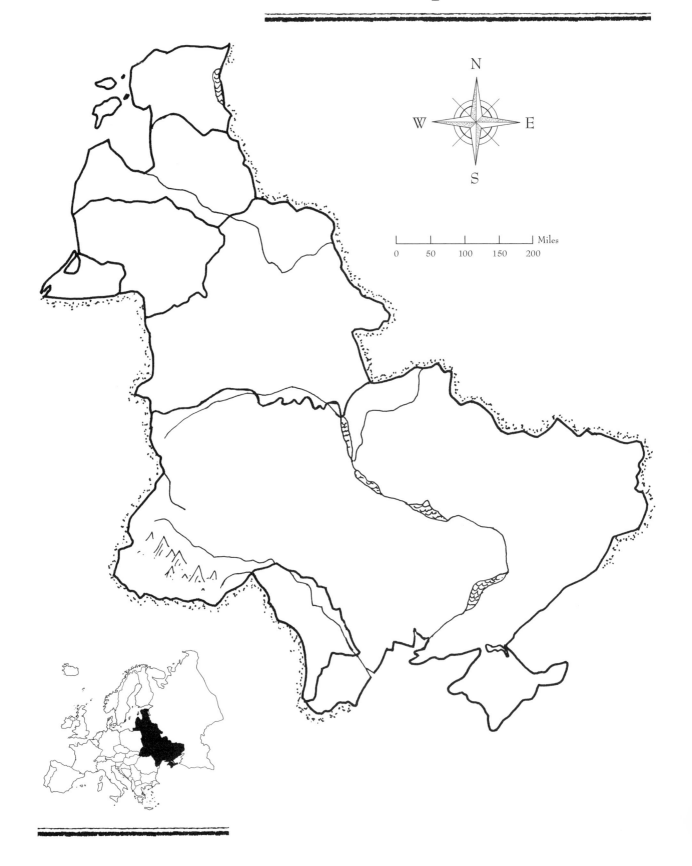

Map It!

Use this worksheet to organize your information as you research the following geographical features of Eastern Europe and the Baltics. This will help you be aware of the locations of all the items you will map before you actually begin so that you can use the space well. If the region doesn't have one of the features listed, simply write "none" on the blank line. Finally, mark each item on the map of the region.

The name of each independent country and its capital city _____

_____

_____

_____

Five other important cities in the region _____

_____

The region's major landforms (e.g., mountain ranges, plains, plateaus) _____

_____

_____

_____

The region's major rivers and river basins _____

_____

_____

_____

The region's major inland bodies of water _____

_____

_____

The region's deserts _____

_____

The region's important islands, peninsulas, and capes _____

_____

_____

Bodies of water that border the region _____

_____

_____

Any other special geographical features _____

_____

Belarus

Gather these facts about Belarus, filling in the blanks.

Capital _____ Type of government _____

Date of independence _____ From _____

Chief of state _____

Head of government _____

Name for citizen (e.g., Canadian) _____

Current population _____ World rank in population _____

Life expectancy_____ men _____ women Literacy_____ % male _____ % female

Ethnic groups _____

Major religions _____

Major languages _____

Land area _____ Water area _____ World rank in area _____

Five largest cities and their populations _____

_____

Bordering nations _____

_____

Climate _____

Terrain _____

Highest point and its elevation _____

Lowest point and its elevation _____

GDP_____ Per capita GDP _____ World rank in GDP _____

Major natural resources _____

Major industries _____

Chief agricultural products _____

Major exports _____

Major imports _____

Estonia

Gather these facts about Estonia, filling in the blanks.

Capital _____ Type of government _____

Date of independence _____ From _____

Chief of state _____

Head of government _____

Name for citizen (e.g., Canadian) _____

Current population _____ World rank in population _____

Life expectancy _____ men _____ women   Literacy _____ % male _____ % female

Ethnic groups _____

Major religions _____

Major languages _____

Land area _____ Water area _____ World rank in area _____

Five largest cities and their populations _____

_____

Bordering nations _____

_____

Climate _____

Terrain _____

Highest point and its elevation _____

Lowest point and its elevation _____

GDP _____ Per capita GDP _____ World rank in GDP _____

Major natural resources _____

Major industries _____

Chief agricultural products _____

Major exports _____

Major imports _____

Latvia

Gather these facts about Latvia, filling in the blanks.

Capital _____ Type of government _____

Date of independence _____ From _____

Chief of state _____

Head of government _____

Name for citizen (e.g., Canadian) _____

Current population _____ World rank in population _____

Life expectancy _____ men _____ women Literacy _____ % male _____ % female

Ethnic groups _____

Major religions _____

Major languages _____

Land area _____ Water area _____ World rank in area _____

Five largest cities and their populations _____

_____

Bordering nations _____

_____

Climate _____

Terrain _____

Highest point and its elevation _____

Lowest point and its elevation _____

GDP _____ Per capita GDP _____ World rank in GDP _____

Major natural resources _____

Major industries _____

Chief agricultural products _____

Major exports _____

Major imports _____

Lithuania

Gather these facts about Lithuania, filling in the blanks.

Capital _____ Type of government _____

Date of independence _____ From _____

Chief of state _____

Head of government _____

Name for citizen (e.g., Canadian) _____

Current population _____ World rank in population _____

Life expectancy _____ men _____ women Literacy _____ % male _____ % female

Ethnic groups _____

Major religions _____

Major languages _____

Land area _____ Water area _____ World rank in area _____

Five largest cities and their populations _____

_____

Bordering nations _____

_____

Climate _____

Terrain _____

Highest point and its elevation _____

Lowest point and its elevation _____

GDP _____ Per capita GDP _____ World rank in GDP _____

Major natural resources _____

Major industries _____

Chief agricultural products _____

Major exports _____

Major imports _____

Moldova

Gather these facts about Moldova, filling in the blanks.

Capital _____ Type of government ___ _____

Date of independence _____ From _____

Chief of state _____

Head of government _____

Name for citizen (e.g., Canadian) _____

Current population _____ World rank in population _____

Life expectancy _____ men _____ women Literacy _____ % male _____ % female

Ethnic groups _____

Major religions _____

Major languages _____

Land area _____ Water area _____ World rank in area _____

Five largest cities and their populations _____

_____

Bordering nations _____

_____

Climate _____

Terrain _____

Highest point and its elevation _____

Lowest point and its elevation _____

GDP _____ Per capita GDP _____ World rank in GDP _____

Major natural resources _____

Major industries _____

Chief agricultural products _____

Major exports _____

Major imports _____

Ukraine

Gather these facts about Ukraine, filling in the blanks.

Capital _____ Type of government _____

Date of independence _____ From _____

Chief of state _____

Head of government _____

Name for citizen (e.g., Canadian) _____

Current population _____ World rank in population _____

Life expectancy _____ men _____ women Literacy _____ % male _____ % female

Ethnic groups _____

Major religions _____

Major languages _____

Land area _____ Water area _____ World rank in area _____

Five largest cities and their populations _____

_____

Bordering nations _____

_____

Climate _____

Terrain _____

Highest point and its elevation _____

Lowest point and its elevation _____

GDP _____ Per capita GDP _____ World rank in GDP _____

Major natural resources _____

Major industries _____

Chief agricultural products _____

Major exports _____

Major imports _____

Russia

Map It!

Use this worksheet to organize your information as you research the following geographical features of Russia. This will help you be aware of the locations of all the items you will map before you actually begin so that you can use the space well. If Russia doesn't have one of the features listed, simply write "none" on the blank line. Finally, mark each item on the map of the country.

Russia's capital city _____

Russia's five largest cities _____

_____

Russia's major landforms (e.g., mountain ranges, plains, plateaus) _____

_____

_____

_____

Russia's highest and lowest points and their elevations _____

_____

Russia's major rivers and river basins _____

_____

_____

_____

Russia's major inland bodies of water _____

_____

_____

Russia's deserts _____

_____

Russia's important islands, peninsulas, and capes _____

_____

_____

Bodies of water that border Russia _____

_____

_____

Any other special geographical features _____

_____

Russia

Gather these facts about Russia, filling in the blanks.

Capital _____ Type of government _____

Date of independence _____ From _____

Chief of state _____

Head of government _____

Name for citizen (e.g., Canadian) _____

Current population _____ World rank in population _____

Life expectancy _____ men _____ women Literacy _____ % male _____ % female

Ethnic groups _____

Major religions _____

Major languages _____

Land area _____ Water area _____ World rank in area _____

Five largest cities and their populations _____

_____

Bordering nations _____

_____

Climate _____

Terrain _____

Highest point and its elevation _____

Lowest point and its elevation _____

GDP _____ Per capita GDP _____ World rank in GDP _____

Major natural resources _____

Major industries _____

Chief agricultural products _____

Major exports _____

Major imports _____

Asia

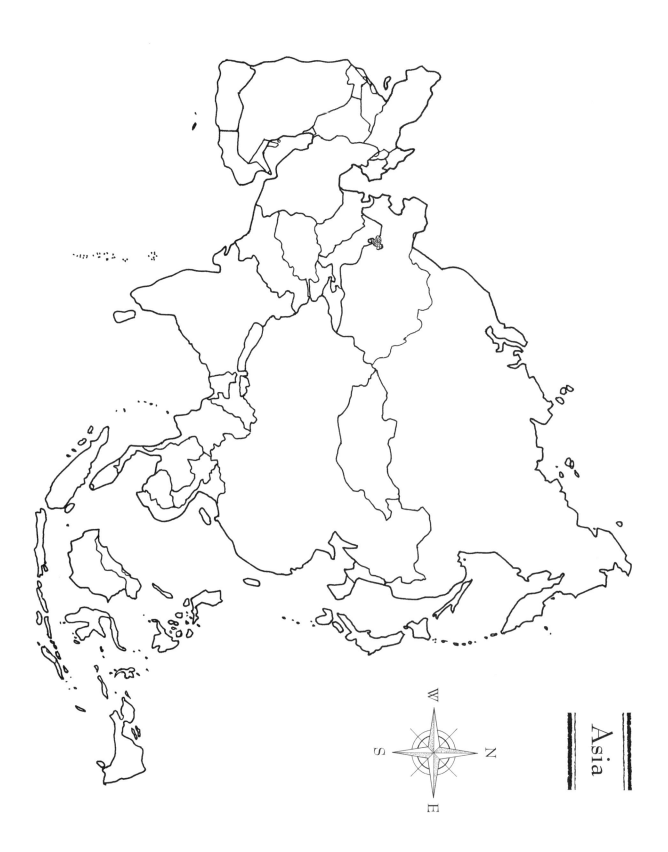

Asia

Asia

Gather these facts about the continent of Asia, filling in the blanks.

Total land area _____ Rank in area _____ of 7

Total population _____ Rank in population _____ of 7

Major languages _____

Major religions _____

Major natural resources _____

Longest river _____

Highest mountain _____

Lowest point _____

Largest lake _____

Biggest desert _____

Biggest island _____

Three largest cities _____

Number of independent countries _____

Largest country _____

Smallest country _____

Most populous country _____

Least populous country _____

Most densely populated country _____

Least densely populated country _____

Two countries partly in Europe and partly in Asia _____

Disputed territories and borders in Asia _____

_____

Map It!

On the political map of Asia, label each independent country and its capital. Then use colored pencils to make each country a different color than the countries that border it.

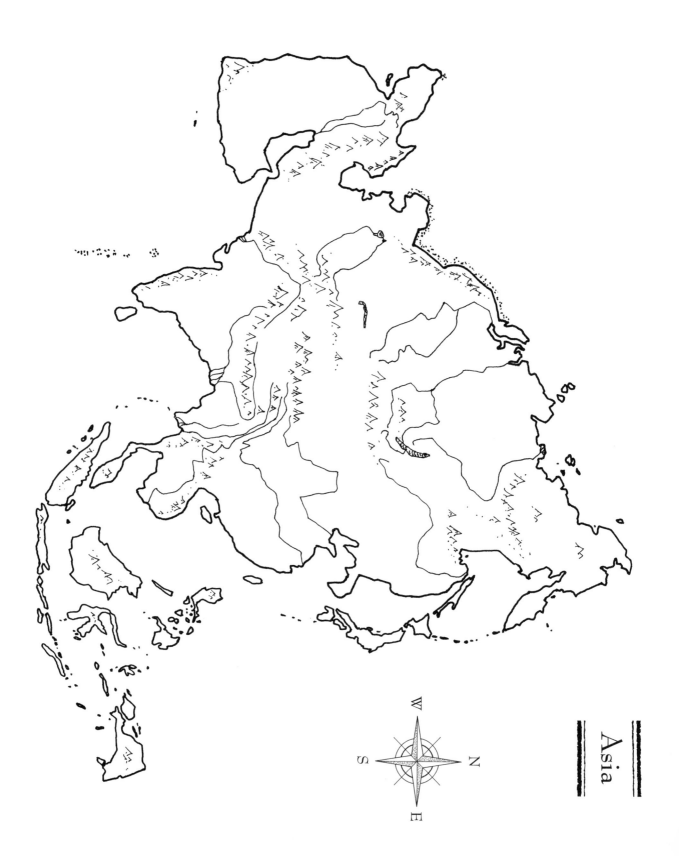

Asia

Map It!

Use this worksheet to organize your information as you research the following geographical features of Asia. This will help you be aware of the locations of all the items you will map before you actually begin so that you can use the space well. Finally, mark each item on the physical map of the continent.

Asia's major landforms (e.g., mountain ranges, plains, plateaus) _____

_____

_____

Asia's major rivers and river basins _____

_____

_____

Asia's major inland bodies of water _____

_____

_____

Asia's deserts _____

_____

_____

Asia's major islands, peninsulas, and capes _____

_____

_____

Bodies of water that border Asia _____

_____

_____

Asia's highest and lowest points and their elevations _____

_____

Any of the following lines of latitude that intersect Asia: Arctic Circle, Tropic of Cancer, Equator, Tropic of Capricorn, Antarctic Circle _____

_____

Any other special geographical features _____

_____

_____

Southwest Asia

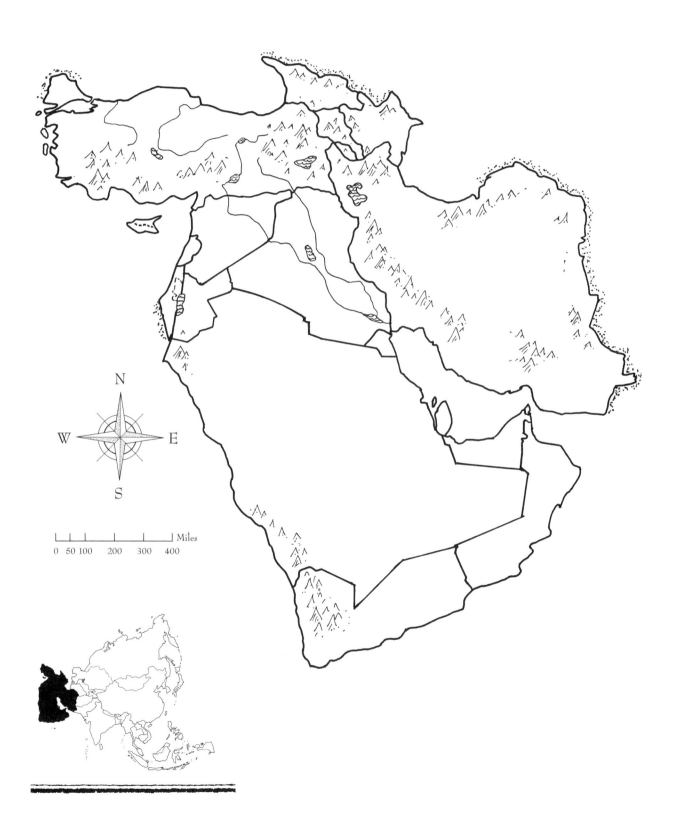

N
W   E
S

⊢—⊢—⊢———⊢———⊢ Miles
0 50 100   200   300   400

Map It!

Use this worksheet to organize your information as you research the following geographical features of Southwest Asia. This will help you be aware of the locations of all the items you will map before you actually begin so that you can use the space well. If the region doesn't have one of the features listed, simply write "none" on the blank line. Finally, mark each item on the map of the region.

The name of each independent country and its capital city _____

_____

_____

_____

_____

_____

_____

The region's major landforms (e.g., mountain ranges, plains, plateaus) _____

_____

_____

_____

The region's major rivers and river basins _____

_____

_____

_____

The region's major inland bodies of water _____

_____

_____

The region's deserts _____

_____

The region's important islands, peninsulas, and capes _____

_____

_____

Bodies of water that border the region _____

_____

_____

Any other special geographical features _____

_____

Armenia

Gather these facts about Armenia, filling in the blanks.

Capital _____ Type of government _____

Date of independence _____ From _____

Chief of state _____

Head of government _____

Name for citizen (e.g., Canadian) _____

Current population _____ World rank in population _____

Life expectancy _____ men _____ women   Literacy _____ % male _____ % female

Ethnic groups _____

Major religions _____

Major languages _____

Land area _____ Water area _____ World rank in area _____

Five largest cities and their populations _____

_____

Bordering nations _____

_____

Climate _____

Terrain _____

Highest point and its elevation _____

Lowest point and its elevation _____

GDP _____ Per capita GDP _____ World rank in GDP _____

Major natural resources _____

Major industries _____

Chief agricultural products _____

Major exports _____

Major imports _____

Azerbaijan

Gather these facts about Azerbaijan, filling in the blanks.

Capital _____ Type of government _____

Date of independence _____ From _____

Chief of state _____

Head of government _____

Name for citizen (e.g., Canadian) _____

Current population _____ World rank in population _____

Life expectancy _____ men _____ women Literacy _____ % male _____ % female

Ethnic groups _____

Major religions _____

Major languages _____

Land area _____ Water area _____ World rank in area _____

Five largest cities and their populations _____

_____

Bordering nations _____

_____

Climate _____

Terrain _____

Highest point and its elevation _____

Lowest point and its elevation _____

GDP _____ Per capita GDP _____ World rank in GDP _____

Major natural resources _____

Major industries _____

Chief agricultural products _____

Major exports _____

Major imports _____

Bahrain

Gather these facts about Bahrain, filling in the blanks.

Capital _____ Type of government _____

Date of independence _____ From _____

Chief of state _____

Head of government _____

Name for citizen (e.g., Canadian) _____

Current population _____ World rank in population _____

Life expectancy _____ men _____ women Literacy _____ % male _____ % female

Ethnic groups _____

Major religions _____

Major languages _____

Land area _____ Water area _____ World rank in area _____

Five largest cities and their populations _____

_____

Bordering nations _____

_____

Climate _____

Terrain _____

Highest point and its elevation _____

Lowest point and its elevation _____

GDP _____ Per capita GDP _____ World rank in GDP _____

Major natural resources _____

Major industries _____

Chief agricultural products _____

Major exports _____

Major imports _____

Cyprus

Gather these facts about Cyprus, filling in the blanks.

Capital _____ Type of government _____

Date of independence _____ From _____

Chief of state _____

Head of government _____

Name for citizen (e.g., Canadian) _____

Current population _____ World rank in population _____

Life expectancy _____ men _____ women   Literacy _____ % male _____ % female

Ethnic groups _____

Major religions _____

Major languages _____

Land area _____ Water area _____ World rank in area _____

Five largest cities and their populations _____

_____

Bordering nations _____

_____

Climate _____

Terrain _____

Highest point and its elevation _____

Lowest point and its elevation _____

GDP _____ Per capita GDP _____ World rank in GDP _____

Major natural resources _____

Major industries _____

Chief agricultural products _____

Major exports _____

Major imports _____

239

Georgia

Gather these facts about Georgia, filling in the blanks.

Capital _____ Type of government _____

Date of independence _____ From _____

Chief of state _____

Head of government _____

Name for citizen (e.g., Canadian) _____

Current population _____ World rank in population _____

Life expectancy_____ men _____ women Literacy_____ % male _____ % female

Ethnic groups _____

Major religions _____

Major languages _____

Land area _____ Water area _____ World rank in area _____

Five largest cities and their populations _____

_____

Bordering nations _____

_____

Climate _____

Terrain _____

Highest point and its elevation _____

Lowest point and its elevation _____

GDP_____ Per capita GDP _____ World rank in GDP _____

Major natural resources _____

Major industries _____

Chief agricultural products _____

Major exports _____

Major imports _____

Iran

Gather these facts about Iran, filling in the blanks.

Capital _____ Type of government _____

Date of independence _____ From _____

Chief of state _____

Head of government _____

Name for citizen (e.g., Canadian) _____

Current population _____ World rank in population _____

Life expectancy _____ men _____ women   Literacy _____ % male _____ % female

Ethnic groups _____

Major religions _____

Major languages _____

Land area _____ Water area _____ World rank in area _____

Five largest cities and their populations _____

_____

Bordering nations _____

_____

Climate _____

Terrain _____

Highest point and its elevation _____

Lowest point and its elevation _____

GDP _____ Per capita GDP _____ World rank in GDP _____

Major natural resources _____

Major industries _____

Chief agricultural products _____

Major exports _____

Major imports _____

Iraq

Gather these facts about Iraq, filling in the blanks.

Capital _____ Type of government _____

Date of independence _____ From _____

Chief of state _____

Head of government _____

Name for citizen (e.g., Canadian) _____

Current population _____ World rank in population _____

Life expectancy _____ men _____ women Literacy _____ % male _____ % female

Ethnic groups _____

Major religions _____

Major languages _____

Land area _____ Water area _____ World rank in area _____

Five largest cities and their populations _____

_____

Bordering nations _____

_____

Climate _____

Terrain _____

Highest point and its elevation _____

Lowest point and its elevation _____

GDP _____ Per capita GDP _____ World rank in GDP _____

Major natural resources _____

Major industries _____

Chief agricultural products _____

Major exports _____

Major imports _____

Israel

Gather these facts about Israel, filling in the blanks.

Capital _____ Type of government _____

Date of independence _____ From _____

Chief of state _____

Head of government _____

Name for citizen (e.g., Canadian) _____

Current population _____ World rank in population _____

Life expectancy _____ men _____ women   Literacy _____ % male _____ % female

Ethnic groups _____

Major religions _____

Major languages _____

Land area _____ Water area _____ World rank in area _____

Five largest cities and their populations _____

_____

Bordering nations _____

_____

Climate _____

Terrain _____

Highest point and its elevation _____

Lowest point and its elevation _____

GDP _____ Per capita GDP _____ World rank in GDP _____

Major natural resources _____

Major industries _____

Chief agricultural products _____

Major exports _____

Major imports _____

Jordan

Gather these facts about Jordan, filling in the blanks.

Capital _____ Type of government _____

Date of independence _____ From _____

Chief of state _____

Head of government _____

Name for citizen (e.g., Canadian) _____

Current population _____ World rank in population _____

Life expectancy _____ men _____ women Literacy _____ % male _____ % female

Ethnic groups _____

Major religions _____

Major languages _____

Land area _____ Water area _____ World rank in area _____

Five largest cities and their populations _____

_____

Bordering nations _____

_____

Climate _____

Terrain _____

Highest point and its elevation _____

Lowest point and its elevation _____

GDP _____ Per capita GDP _____ World rank in GDP _____

Major natural resources _____

Major industries _____

Chief agricultural products _____

Major exports _____

Major imports _____

Kuwait

Gather these facts about Kuwait, filling in the blanks.

Capital _____ Type of government _____

Date of independence _____ From _____

Chief of state _____

Head of government _____

Name for citizen (e.g., Canadian) _____

Current population _____ World rank in population _____

Life expectancy _____ men _____ women   Literacy _____ % male _____ % female

Ethnic groups _____

Major religions _____

Major languages _____

Land area _____ Water area _____ World rank in area _____

Five largest cities and their populations _____

_____

Bordering nations _____

_____

Climate _____

Terrain _____

Highest point and its elevation _____

Lowest point and its elevation _____

GDP _____ Per capita GDP _____ World rank in GDP _____

Major natural resources _____

Major industries _____

Chief agricultural products _____

Major exports _____

Major imports _____

Lebanon

Gather these facts about Lebanon, filling in the blanks.

Capital _____ Type of government _____

Date of independence _____ From _____

Chief of state _____

Head of government _____

Name for citizen (e.g., Canadian) _____

Current population _____ World rank in population _____

Life expectancy _____ men _____ women Literacy _____ % male _____ % female

Ethnic groups _____

Major religions _____

Major languages _____

Land area _____ Water area _____ World rank in area _____

Five largest cities and their populations _____

_____

Bordering nations _____

_____

Climate _____

Terrain _____

Highest point and its elevation _____

Lowest point and its elevation _____

GDP _____ Per capita GDP _____ World rank in GDP _____

Major natural resources _____

Major industries _____

Chief agricultural products _____

Major exports _____

Major imports _____

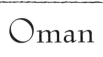

Oman

Gather these facts about Oman, filling in the blanks.

Capital _____ Type of government _____

Date of independence _____ From _____

Chief of state _____

Head of government _____

Name for citizen (e.g., Canadian) _____

Current population _____ World rank in population _____

Life expectancy _____ men _____ women Literacy _____ % male _____ % female

Ethnic groups _____

Major religions _____

Major languages _____

Land area _____ Water area _____ World rank in area _____

Five largest cities and their populations _____

_____

Bordering nations _____

_____

Climate _____

Terrain _____

Highest point and its elevation _____

Lowest point and its elevation _____

GDP _____ Per capita GDP _____ World rank in GDP _____

Major natural resources _____

Major industries _____

Chief agricultural products _____

Major exports _____

Major imports _____

Qatar

Gather these facts about Qatar, filling in the blanks.

Capital _____ Type of government _____

Date of independence _____ From _____

Chief of state _____

Head of government _____

Name for citizen (e.g., Canadian) _____

Current population _____ World rank in population _____

Life expectancy _____ men _____ women   Literacy _____ % male _____ % female

Ethnic groups _____

Major religions _____

Major languages _____

Land area _____ Water area _____ World rank in area _____

Five largest cities and their populations _____

_____

Bordering nations _____

_____

Climate _____

Terrain _____

Highest point and its elevation _____

Lowest point and its elevation _____

GDP _____ Per capita GDP _____ World rank in GDP _____

Major natural resources _____

Major industries _____

Chief agricultural products _____

Major exports _____

Major imports _____

Saudi Arabia

Gather these facts about Saudi Arabia, filling in the blanks.

Capital _____ Type of government _____

Date of independence _____ From _____

Chief of state _____

Head of government _____

Name for citizen (e.g., Canadian) _____

Current population _____ World rank in population _____

Life expectancy _____ men _____ women Literacy _____ % male _____ % female

Ethnic groups _____

Major religions _____

Major languages _____

Land area _____ Water area _____ World rank in area _____

Five largest cities and their populations _____

_____

Bordering nations _____

_____

Climate _____

Terrain _____

Highest point and its elevation _____

Lowest point and its elevation _____

GDP _____ Per capita GDP _____ World rank in GDP _____

Major natural resources _____

Major industries _____

Chief agricultural products _____

Major exports _____

Major imports _____

Syria

Gather these facts about Syria, filling in the blanks.

Capital _____ Type of government _____

Date of independence _____ From _____

Chief of state _____

Head of government _____

Name for citizen (e.g., Canadian) _____

Current population _____ World rank in population _____

Life expectancy _____ men _____ women   Literacy _____ % male _____ % female

Ethnic groups _____

Major religions _____

Major languages _____

Land area _____ Water area _____ World rank in area _____

Five largest cities and their populations _____

_____

Bordering nations _____

_____

Climate _____

Terrain _____

Highest point and its elevation _____

Lowest point and its elevation _____

GDP _____ Per capita GDP _____ World rank in GDP _____

Major natural resources _____

Major industries _____

Chief agricultural products _____

Major exports _____

Major imports _____

Turkey

Gather these facts about Turkey, filling in the blanks.

Capital _____ Type of government _____

Date of independence _____ From _____

Chief of state _____

Head of government _____

Name for citizen (e.g., Canadian) _____

Current population _____ World rank in population _____

Life expectancy _____ men _____ women Literacy _____ % male _____ % female

Ethnic groups _____

Major religions _____

Major languages _____

Land area _____ Water area _____ World rank in area _____

Five largest cities and their populations _____

_____

Bordering nations _____

_____

Climate _____

Terrain _____

Highest point and its elevation _____

Lowest point and its elevation _____

GDP _____ Per capita GDP _____ World rank in GDP _____

Major natural resources _____

Major industries _____

Chief agricultural products _____

Major exports _____

Major imports _____

United Arab Emirates

Gather these facts about United Arab Emirates, filling in the blanks.

Capital _____ Type of government _____

Date of independence _____ From _____

Chief of state _____

Head of government _____

Name for citizen (e.g., Canadian) _____

Current population _____ World rank in population _____

Life expectancy _____ men _____ women Literacy _____ % male _____ % female

Ethnic groups _____

Major religions _____

Major languages _____

Land area _____ Water area _____ World rank in area _____

Five largest cities and their populations _____

_____

Bordering nations _____

_____

Climate _____

Terrain _____

Highest point and its elevation _____

Lowest point and its elevation _____

GDP _____ Per capita GDP _____ World rank in GDP _____

Major natural resources _____

Major industries _____

Chief agricultural products _____

Major exports _____

Major imports _____

Yemen

Gather these facts about Yemen, filling in the blanks.

Capital _____ Type of government _____

Date of independence _____ From _____

Chief of state _____

Head of government _____

Name for citizen (e.g., Canadian) _____

Current population _____ World rank in population _____

Life expectancy _____ men _____ women Literacy _____ % male _____ % female

Ethnic groups _____

Major religions _____

Major languages _____

Land area _____ Water area _____ World rank in area _____

Five largest cities and their populations _____

_____

Bordering nations _____

_____

Climate _____

Terrain _____

Highest point and its elevation _____

Lowest point and its elevation _____

GDP _____ Per capita GDP _____ World rank in GDP _____

Major natural resources _____

Major industries _____

Chief agricultural products _____

Major exports _____

Major imports _____

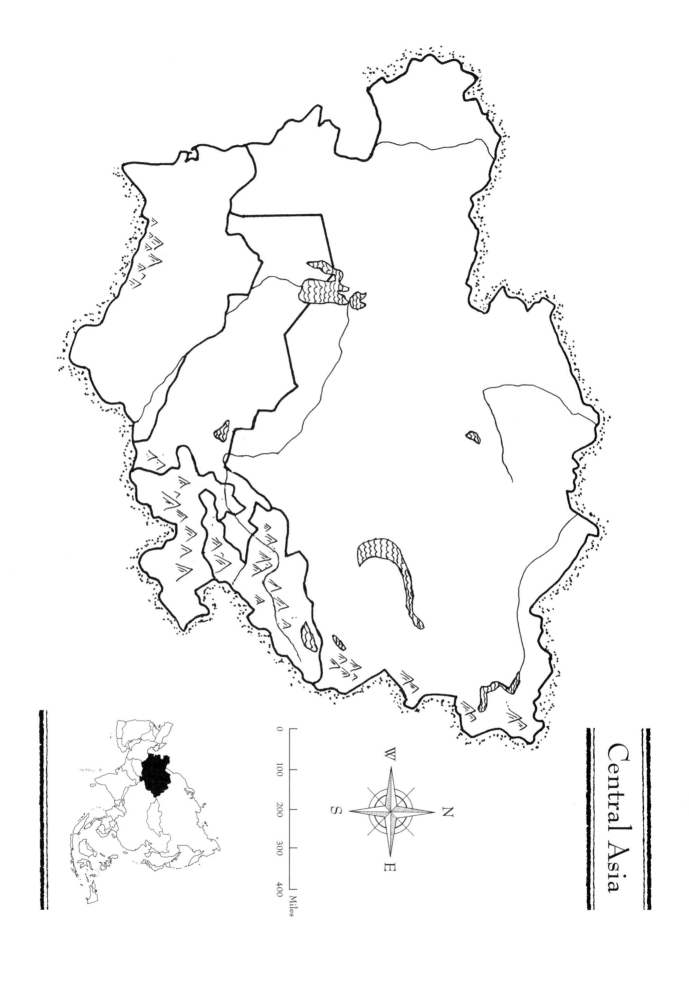

Central Asia

Map It!

Use this worksheet to organize your information as you research the following geographical features of Central Asia. This will help you be aware of the locations of all the items you will map before you actually begin so that you can use the space well. If the region doesn't have one of the features listed, simply write "none" on the blank line. Finally, mark each item on the map of the region.

The name of each independent country and its capital city _____
_____
_____
_____

Five other important cities in the region _____
_____

The region's major landforms (e.g., mountain ranges, plains, plateaus) _____
_____
_____
_____

The region's major rivers and river basins _____
_____
_____
_____

The region's major inland bodies of water _____
_____
_____

The region's deserts _____
_____

The region's important islands, peninsulas, and capes _____
_____
_____

Bodies of water that border the region _____
_____
_____

Any other special geographical features _____
_____

Kazakhstan

Gather these facts about Kazakhstan, filling in the blanks.

Capital _____ Type of government _____

Date of independence _____ From _____

Chief of state _____

Head of government _____

Name for citizen (e.g., Canadian) _____

Current population _____ World rank in population _____

Life expectancy _____ men _____ women Literacy _____ % male _____ % female

Ethnic groups _____

Major religions _____

Major languages _____

Land area _____ Water area _____ World rank in area _____

Five largest cities and their populations _____

_____

Bordering nations _____

_____

Climate _____

Terrain _____

Highest point and its elevation _____

Lowest point and its elevation _____

GDP _____ Per capita GDP _____ World rank in GDP _____

Major natural resources _____

Major industries _____

Chief agricultural products _____

Major exports _____

Major imports _____

Kyrgyzstan

Gather these facts about Kyrgyzstan, filling in the blanks.

Capital _____ Type of government _____

Date of independence _____ From _____

Chief of state _____

Head of government _____

Name for citizen (e.g., Canadian) _____

Current population _____ World rank in population _____

Life expectancy _____ men _____ women Literacy _____ % male _____ % female

Ethnic groups _____

Major religions _____

Major languages _____

Land area _____ Water area _____ World rank in area _____

Five largest cities and their populations _____

_____

Bordering nations _____

_____

Climate _____

Terrain _____

Highest point and its elevation _____

Lowest point and its elevation _____

GDP _____ Per capita GDP _____ World rank in GDP _____

Major natural resources _____

Major industries _____

Chief agricultural products _____

Major exports _____

Major imports _____

Tajikistan

Gather these facts about Tajikistan, filling in the blanks.

Capital _____ Type of government _____

Date of independence _____ From _____

Chief of state _____

Head of government _____

Name for citizen (e.g., Canadian) _____

Current population _____ World rank in population _____

Life expectancy _____ men _____ women Literacy _____ % male _____ % female

Ethnic groups _____

Major religions _____

Major languages _____

Land area _____ Water area _____ World rank in area _____

Five largest cities and their populations _____

_____

Bordering nations _____

_____

Climate _____

Terrain _____

Highest point and its elevation _____

Lowest point and its elevation _____

GDP _____ Per capita GDP _____ World rank in GDP _____

Major natural resources _____

Major industries _____

Chief agricultural products _____

Major exports _____

Major imports _____

Turkmenistan

Gather these facts about Turkmenistan, filling in the blanks.

Capital _____ Type of government _____

Date of independence _____ From _____

Chief of state _____

Head of government _____

Name for citizen (e.g., Canadian) _____

Current population _____ World rank in population _____

Life expectancy _____ men _____ women   Literacy _____ % male _____ % female

Ethnic groups _____

Major religions _____

Major languages _____

Land area _____ Water area _____ World rank in area _____

Five largest cities and their populations _____

_____

Bordering nations _____

_____

Climate _____

Terrain _____

Highest point and its elevation _____

Lowest point and its elevation _____

GDP _____ Per capita GDP _____ World rank in GDP _____

Major natural resources _____

Major industries _____

Chief agricultural products _____

Major exports _____

Major imports _____

Uzbekistan

Gather these facts about Uzbekistan, filling in the blanks.

Capital _____ Type of government _____

Date of independence _____ From _____

Chief of state _____

Head of government _____

Name for citizen (e.g., Canadian) _____

Current population _____ World rank in population _____

Life expectancy _____ men _____ women   Literacy _____ % male _____ % female

Ethnic groups _____

Major religions _____

Major languages _____

Land area _____ Water area _____ World rank in area _____

Five largest cities and their populations _____

_____

Bordering nations _____

_____

Climate _____

Terrain _____

Highest point and its elevation _____

Lowest point and its elevation _____

GDP _____ Per capita GDP _____ World rank in GDP _____

Major natural resources _____

Major industries _____

Chief agricultural products _____

Major exports _____

Major imports _____

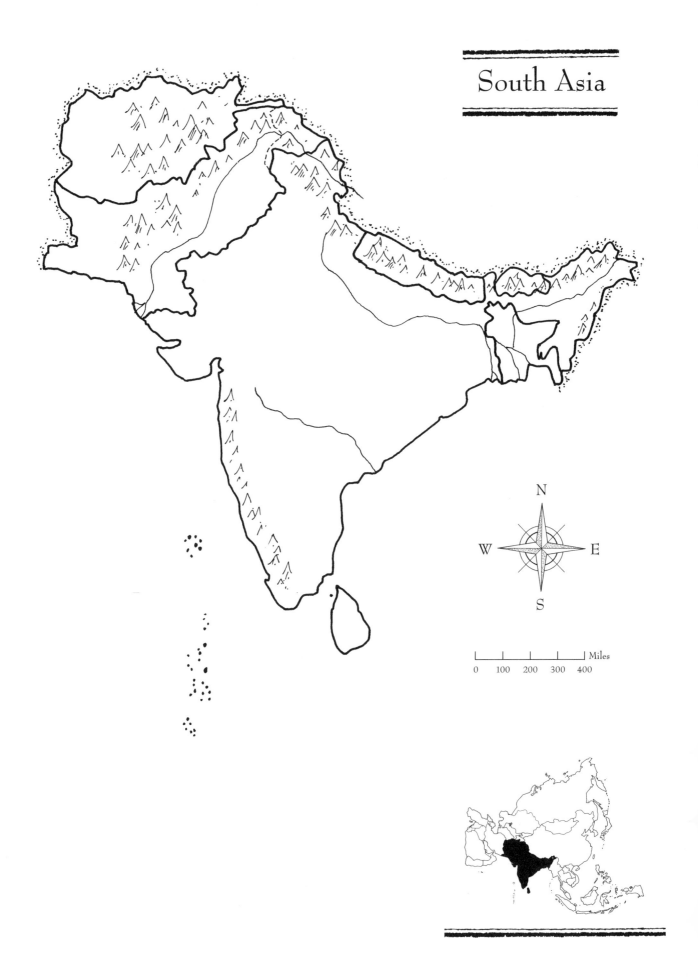

South Asia

Map It!

Use this worksheet to organize your information as you research the following geographical features of South Asia. This will help you be aware of the locations of all the items you will map before you actually begin so that you can use the space well. If the region doesn't have one of the features listed, simply write "none" on the blank line. Finally, mark each item on the map of the region.

The name of each independent country and its capital city _____
_____
_____
_____

Five other important cities in the region _____
_____

The region's major landforms (e.g., mountain ranges, plains, plateaus) _____
_____
_____
_____

The region's major rivers and river basins _____
_____
_____
_____

The region's major inland bodies of water _____
_____
_____

The region's deserts _____
_____

The region's important islands, peninsulas, and capes _____
_____
_____

Bodies of water that border the region _____
_____
_____

Any other special geographical features _____
_____

Afghanistan

Gather these facts about Afghanistan, filling in the blanks.

Capital _____ Type of government _____

Date of independence _____ From _____

Chief of state _____

Head of government _____

Name for citizen (e.g., Canadian) _____

Current population _____ World rank in population _____

Life expectancy _____ men _____ women Literacy _____ % male _____ % female

Ethnic groups _____

Major religions _____

Major languages _____

Land area _____ Water area _____ World rank in area _____

Five largest cities and their populations _____

_____

Bordering nations _____

_____

Climate _____

Terrain _____

Highest point and its elevation _____

Lowest point and its elevation _____

GDP _____ Per capita GDP _____ World rank in GDP _____

Major natural resources _____

Major industries _____

Chief agricultural products _____

Major exports _____

Major imports _____

Bangladesh

Gather these facts about Bangladesh, filling in the blanks.

Capital _____ Type of government _____

Date of independence _____ From _____

Chief of state _____

Head of government _____

Name for citizen (e.g., Canadian) _____

Current population _____ World rank in population _____

Life expectancy_____ men _____ women Literacy_____ % male _____ % female

Ethnic groups _____

Major religions _____

Major languages _____

Land area _____ Water area _____ World rank in area _____

Five largest cities and their populations _____

_____

Bordering nations _____

_____

Climate _____

Terrain _____

Highest point and its elevation _____

Lowest point and its elevation _____

GDP_____ Per capita GDP _____ World rank in GDP _____

Major natural resources _____

Major industries _____

Chief agricultural products _____

Major exports _____

Major imports _____

Bhutan

Gather these facts about Bhutan, filling in the blanks.

Capital _____ Type of government _____

Date of independence _____ From _____

Chief of state _____

Head of government _____

Name for citizen (e.g., Canadian) _____

Current population _____ World rank in population _____

Life expectancy _____ men _____ women Literacy _____ % male _____ % female

Ethnic groups _____

Major religions _____

Major languages _____

Land area _____ Water area _____ World rank in area _____

Five largest cities and their populations _____

_____

Bordering nations _____

_____

Climate _____

Terrain _____

Highest point and its elevation _____

Lowest point and its elevation _____

GDP _____ Per capita GDP _____ World rank in GDP _____

Major natural resources _____

Major industries _____

Chief agricultural products _____

Major exports _____

Major imports _____

India

Gather these facts about India, filling in the blanks.

Capital _____ Type of government _____

Date of independence _____ From _____

Chief of state _____

Head of government _____

Name for citizen (e.g., Canadian) _____

Current population _____ World rank in population _____

Life expectancy _____ men _____ women Literacy _____ % male _____ % female

Ethnic groups _____

Major religions _____

Major languages _____

Land area _____ Water area _____ World rank in area _____

Five largest cities and their populations _____

_____

Bordering nations _____

_____

Climate _____

Terrain _____

Highest point and its elevation _____

Lowest point and its elevation _____

GDP _____ Per capita GDP _____ World rank in GDP _____

Major natural resources _____

Major industries _____

Chief agricultural products _____

Major exports _____

Major imports _____

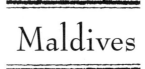

Maldives

Gather these facts about Maldives, filling in the blanks.

Capital _____ Type of government _____

Date of independence _____ From _____

Chief of state _____

Head of government _____

Name for citizen (e.g., Canadian) _____

Current population _____ World rank in population _____

Life expectancy _____ men _____ women Literacy _____ % male _____ % female

Ethnic groups _____

Major religions _____

Major languages _____

Land area _____ Water area _____ World rank in area _____

Five largest cities and their populations _____

_____

Bordering nations _____

_____

Climate _____

Terrain _____

Highest point and its elevation _____

Lowest point and its elevation _____

GDP _____ Per capita GDP _____ World rank in GDP _____

Major natural resources _____

Major industries _____

Chief agricultural products _____

Major exports _____

Major imports _____

Nepal

Gather these facts about Nepal, filling in the blanks.

Capital _____ Type of government _____

Date of independence _____ From _____

Chief of state _____

Head of government _____

Name for citizen (e.g., Canadian) _____

Current population _____ World rank in population _____

Life expectancy _____ men _____ women   Literacy _____ % male _____ % female

Ethnic groups _____

Major religions _____

Major languages _____

Land area _____ Water area _____ World rank in area _____

Five largest cities and their populations _____

_____

Bordering nations _____

_____

Climate _____

Terrain _____

Highest point and its elevation _____

Lowest point and its elevation _____

GDP_____ Per capita GDP _____ World rank in GDP _____

Major natural resources _____

Major industries _____

Chief agricultural products _____

Major exports _____

Major imports _____

Pakistan

Gather these facts about Pakistan, filling in the blanks.

Capital _____ Type of government _____

Date of independence _____ From _____

Chief of state _____

Head of government _____

Name for citizen (e.g., Canadian) _____

Current population _____ World rank in population _____

Life expectancy _____ men _____ women Literacy _____ % male _____ % female

Ethnic groups _____

Major religions _____

Major languages _____

Land area _____ Water area _____ World rank in area _____

Five largest cities and their populations _____

_____

Bordering nations _____

_____

Climate _____

Terrain _____

Highest point and its elevation _____

Lowest point and its elevation _____

GDP _____ Per capita GDP _____ World rank in GDP _____

Major natural resources _____

Major industries _____

Chief agricultural products _____

Major exports _____

Major imports _____

Sri Lanka

Gather these facts about Sri Lanka, filling in the blanks.

Capital _____ Type of government _____

Date of independence _____ From _____

Chief of state _____

Head of government _____

Name for citizen (e.g., Canadian) _____

Current population _____ World rank in population _____

Life expectancy _____ men _____ women Literacy _____ % male _____ % female

Ethnic groups _____

Major religions _____

Major languages _____

Land area _____ Water area _____ World rank in area _____

Five largest cities and their populations _____

_____

Bordering nations _____

_____

Climate _____

Terrain _____

Highest point and its elevation _____

Lowest point and its elevation _____

GDP _____ Per capita GDP _____ World rank in GDP _____

Major natural resources _____

Major industries _____

Chief agricultural products _____

Major exports _____

Major imports _____

S W N E

0
200
400
600
Miles

Map It!

Use this worksheet to organize your information as you research the following geographical features of Mainland East Asia. This will help you be aware of the locations of all the items you will map before you actually begin so that you can use the space well. If the region doesn't have one of the features listed, simply write "none" on the blank line. Finally, mark each item on the map of the region.

The name of each independent country and its capital city _____

_____

_____

_____

Five other important cities in the region _____

_____

The region's major landforms (e.g., mountain ranges, plains, plateaus) _____

_____

_____

_____

The region's major rivers and river basins _____

_____

_____

_____

The region's major inland bodies of water _____

_____

_____

The region's deserts _____

_____

The region's important islands, peninsulas, and capes _____

_____

_____

Bodies of water that border the region _____

_____

_____

Any other special geographical features _____

_____

China

Gather these facts about China, filling in the blanks.

Capital _____ Type of government _____

Date of independence _____ From _____

Chief of state _____

Head of government _____

Name for citizen (e.g., Canadian) _____

Current population _____ World rank in population _____

Life expectancy _____ men _____ women   Literacy _____ % male _____ % female

Ethnic groups _____

Major religions _____

Major languages _____

Land area _____ Water area _____ World rank in area _____

Five largest cities and their populations _____

_____

Bordering nations _____

_____

Climate _____

Terrain _____

Highest point and its elevation _____

Lowest point and its elevation _____

GDP _____ Per capita GDP _____ World rank in GDP _____

Major natural resources _____

Major industries _____

Chief agricultural products _____

Major exports _____

Major imports _____

Mongolia

Gather these facts about Mongolia, filling in the blanks.

Capital _____ Type of government _____

Date of independence _____ From _____

Chief of state _____

Head of government _____

Name for citizen (e.g., Canadian) _____

Current population _____ World rank in population _____

Life expectancy _____ men _____ women   Literacy _____ % male _____ % female

Ethnic groups _____

Major religions _____

Major languages _____

Land area _____ Water area _____ World rank in area _____

Five largest cities and their populations _____

_____

Bordering nations _____

_____

Climate _____

Terrain _____

Highest point and its elevation _____

Lowest point and its elevation _____

GDP _____ Per capita GDP _____ World rank in GDP _____

Major natural resources _____

Major industries _____

Chief agricultural products _____

Major exports _____

Major imports _____

North Korea

Gather these facts about North Korea, filling in the blanks.

Capital _____ Type of government _____

Date of independence _____ From _____

Chief of state _____

Head of government _____

Name for citizen (e.g., Canadian) _____

Current population _____ World rank in population _____

Life expectancy _____ men _____ women Literacy _____ % male _____ % female

Ethnic groups _____

Major religions _____

Major languages _____

Land area _____ Water area _____ World rank in area _____

Five largest cities and their populations _____

_____

Bordering nations _____

_____

Climate _____

Terrain _____

Highest point and its elevation _____

Lowest point and its elevation _____

GDP _____ Per capita GDP _____ World rank in GDP _____

Major natural resources _____

Major industries _____

Chief agricultural products _____

Major exports _____

Major imports _____

South Korea

Gather these facts about South Korea, filling in the blanks.

Capital _____ Type of government _____

Date of independence _____ From _____

Chief of state _____

Head of government _____

Name for citizen (e.g., Canadian) _____

Current population _____ World rank in population _____

Life expectancy _____ men _____ women   Literacy _____ % male _____ % female

Ethnic groups _____

Major religions _____

Major languages _____

Land area _____ Water area _____ World rank in area _____

Five largest cities and their populations _____

_____

Bordering nations _____

_____

Climate _____

Terrain _____

Highest point and its elevation _____

Lowest point and its elevation _____

GDP _____ Per capita GDP _____ World rank in GDP _____

Major natural resources _____

Major industries _____

Chief agricultural products _____

Major exports _____

Major imports _____

Taiwan

Gather these facts about Taiwan, filling in the blanks.

Capital _____ Type of government _____

Date of independence _____ From _____

Chief of state _____

Head of government _____

Name for citizen (e.g., Canadian) _____

Current population _____ World rank in population _____

Life expectancy _____ men _____ women Literacy _____ % male _____ % female

Ethnic groups _____

Major religions _____

Major languages _____

Land area _____ Water area _____ World rank in area _____

Five largest cities and their populations _____

_____

Bordering nations _____

_____

Climate _____

Terrain _____

Highest point and its elevation _____

Lowest point and its elevation _____

GDP _____ Per capita GDP _____ World rank in GDP _____

Major natural resources _____

Major industries _____

Chief agricultural products _____

Major exports _____

Major imports _____

278

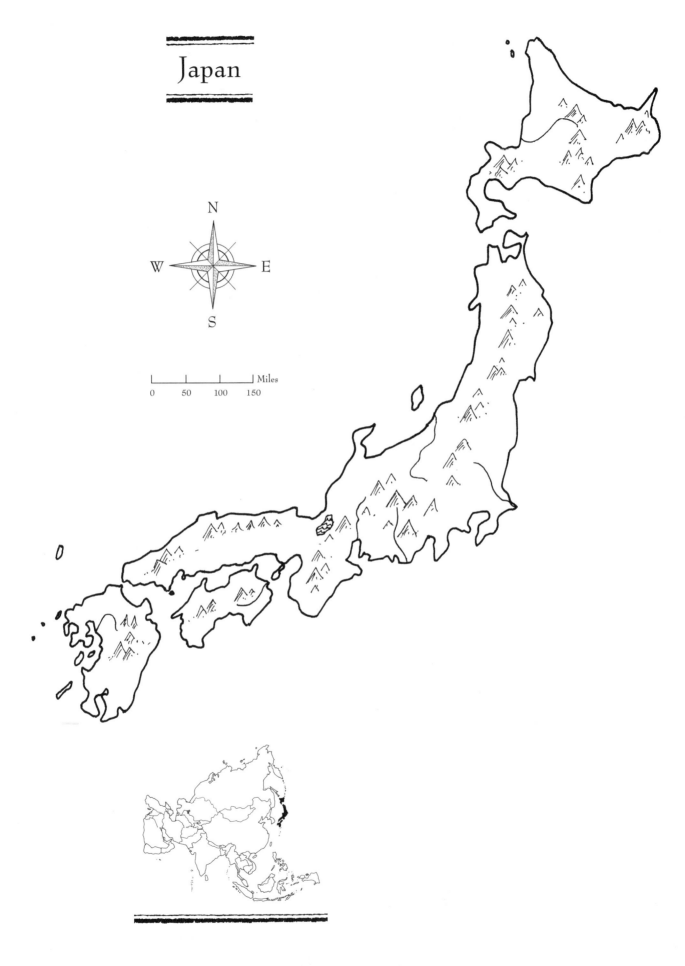

Japan

Map It!

Use this worksheet to organize your information as you research the following geographical features of Japan. This will help you be aware of the locations of all the items you will map before you actually begin so that you can use the space well. If Japan doesn't have one of the features listed, simply write "none" on the blank line. Finally, mark each item on the map of the country.

Japan's capital city _____

Japan's five largest cities _____

_____

Japan's major landforms (e.g., mountain ranges, plains, plateaus) _____

_____

_____

_____

Japan's highest and lowest points and their elevations _____

_____

Japan's major rivers and river basins _____

_____

_____

_____

Japan's major inland bodies of water _____

_____

_____

Japan's deserts _____

_____

Japan's important islands, peninsulas, and capes _____

_____

_____

Bodies of water that border Japan _____

_____

_____

Any other special geographical features _____

_____

Japan

Gather these facts about Japan, filling in the blanks.

Capital _____ Type of government _____

Date of independence _____ From _____

Chief of state _____

Head of government _____

Name for citizen (e.g., Canadian) _____

Current population _____ World rank in population _____

Life expectancy _____ men _____ women   Literacy _____ % male _____ % female

Ethnic groups _____

Major religions _____

Major languages _____

Land area _____ Water area _____ World rank in area _____

Five largest cities and their populations _____

_____

Bordering nations _____

_____

Climate _____

Terrain _____

Highest point and its elevation _____

Lowest point and its elevation _____

GDP _____ Per capita GDP _____ World rank in GDP _____

Major natural resources _____

Major industries _____

Chief agricultural products _____

Major exports _____

Major imports _____

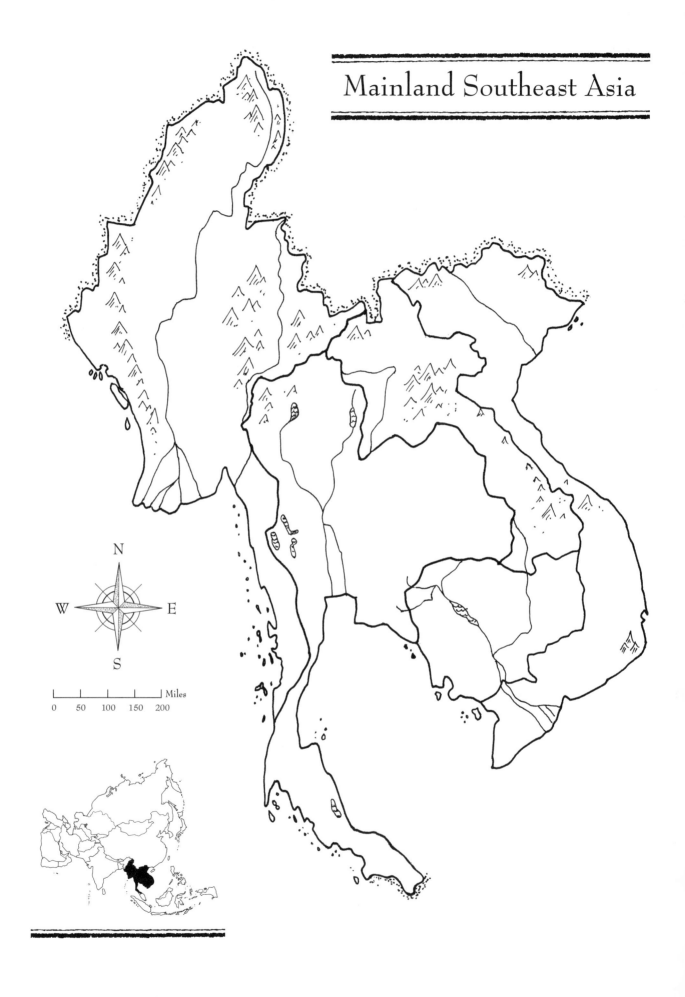

Mainland Southeast Asia

N
W   E
S

|————|————|————|————|————| Miles
0   50   100 150 200

Map It!

Use this worksheet to organize your information as you research the following geographical features of Mainland Southeast Asia. This will help you be aware of the locations of all the items you will map before you actually begin so that you can use the space well. If the region doesn't have one of the features listed, simply write "none" on the blank line. Finally, mark each item on the map of the region.

The name of each independent country and its capital city _____

_____

_____

_____

Five other important cities in the region _____

_____

The region's major landforms (e.g., mountain ranges, plains, plateaus) _____

_____

_____

_____

The region's major rivers and river basins _____

_____

_____

_____

The region's major inland bodies of water _____

_____

_____

The region's deserts _____

_____

The region's important islands, peninsulas, and capes _____

_____

_____

Bodies of water that border the region _____

_____

_____

Any other special geographical features _____

_____

Burma

Gather these facts about Burma, filling in the blanks.

Capital _____ Type of government _____

Date of independence _____ From _____

Chief of state _____

Head of government _____

Name for citizen (e.g., Canadian) _____

Current population _____ World rank in population _____

Life expectancy _____ men _____ women Literacy _____ % male _____ % female

Ethnic groups _____

Major religions _____

Major languages _____

Land area _____ Water area _____ World rank in area _____

Five largest cities and their populations _____

_____

Bordering nations _____

_____

Climate _____

Terrain _____

Highest point and its elevation _____

Lowest point and its elevation _____

GDP _____ Per capita GDP _____ World rank in GDP _____

Major natural resources _____

Major industries _____

Chief agricultural products _____

Major exports _____

Major imports _____

Cambodia

Gather these facts about Cambodia, filling in the blanks.

Capital _____ Type of government _____

Date of independence _____ From _____

Chief of state _____

Head of government _____

Name for citizen (e.g., Canadian) _____

Current population _____ World rank in population _____

Life expectancy _____ men _____ women   Literacy _____ % male _____ % female

Ethnic groups _____

Major religions _____

Major languages _____

Land area _____ Water area _____ World rank in area _____

Five largest cities and their populations _____

_____

Bordering nations _____

_____

Climate _____

Terrain _____

Highest point and its elevation _____

Lowest point and its elevation _____

GDP _____ Per capita GDP _____ World rank in GDP _____

Major natural resources _____

Major industries _____

Chief agricultural products _____

Major exports _____

Major imports _____

Laos

Gather these facts about Laos, filling in the blanks.

Capital _____ Type of government _____

Date of independence _____ From _____

Chief of state _____

Head of government _____

Name for citizen (e.g., Canadian) _____

Current population _____ World rank in population _____

Life expectancy _____ men _____ women   Literacy _____ % male _____ % female

Ethnic groups _____

Major religions _____

Major languages _____

Land area _____ Water area _____ World rank in area _____

Five largest cities and their populations _____

_____

Bordering nations _____

_____

Climate _____

Terrain _____

Highest point and its elevation _____

Lowest point and its elevation _____

GDP _____ Per capita GDP _____ World rank in GDP _____

Major natural resources _____

Major industries _____

Chief agricultural products _____

Major exports _____

Major imports _____

Thailand

Gather these facts about Thailand, filling in the blanks.

Capital _____ Type of government _____

Date of independence _____ From _____

Chief of state _____

Head of government _____

Name for citizen (e.g., Canadian) _____

Current population _____ World rank in population _____

Life expectancy _____ men _____ women   Literacy _____ % male _____ % female

Ethnic groups _____

Major religions _____

Major languages _____

Land area _____ Water area _____ World rank in area _____

Five largest cities and their populations _____

_____

Bordering nations _____

_____

Climate _____

Terrain _____

Highest point and its elevation _____

Lowest point and its elevation _____

GDP_____ Per capita GDP _____ World rank in GDP _____

Major natural resources _____

Major industries _____

Chief agricultural products _____

Major exports _____

Major imports _____

Vietnam

Gather these facts about Vietnam, filling in the blanks.

Capital _____ Type of government _____

Date of independence _____ From _____

Chief of state _____

Head of government _____

Name for citizen (e.g., Canadian) _____

Current population _____ World rank in population _____

Life expectancy _____ men _____ women   Literacy _____ % male _____ % female

Ethnic groups _____

Major religions _____

Major languages _____

Land area _____ Water area _____ World rank in area _____

Five largest cities and their populations _____

_____

Bordering nations _____

_____

Climate _____

Terrain _____

Highest point and its elevation _____

Lowest point and its elevation _____

GDP _____ Per capita GDP _____ World rank in GDP _____

Major natural resources _____

Major industries _____

Chief agricultural products _____

Major exports _____

Major imports _____

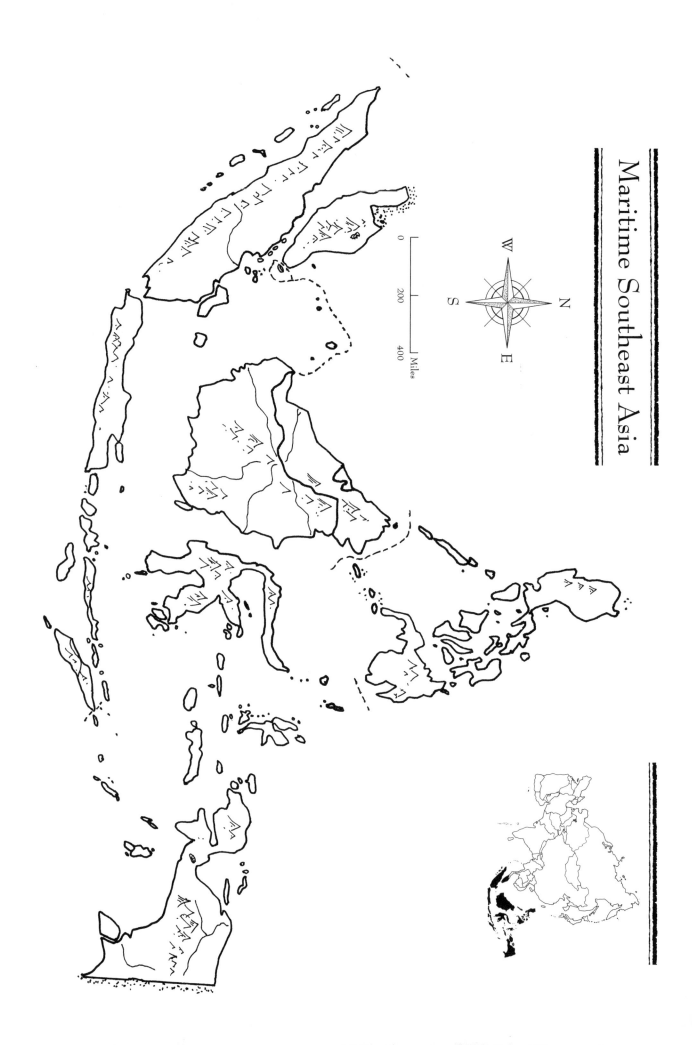

Maritime Southeast Asia

W
N
S
E

0
200
400
Miles

Map It!

Use this worksheet to organize your information as you research the following geographical features of Maritime Southeast Asia. This will help you be aware of the locations of all the items you will map before you actually begin so that you can use the space well. If the region doesn't have one of the features listed, simply write "none" on the blank line. Finally, mark each item on the map of the region.

The name of each independent country and its capital city _____

_____

_____

_____

Five other important cities in the region _____

_____

The region's major landforms (e.g., mountain ranges, plains, plateaus) _____

_____

_____

_____

The region's major rivers and river basins _____

_____

_____

_____

The region's major inland bodies of water _____

_____

_____

The region's deserts _____

_____

The region's important islands, peninsulas, and capes _____

_____

_____

Bodies of water that border the region _____

_____

_____

Any other special geographical features _____

_____

Brunei

Gather these facts about Brunei, filling in the blanks.

Capital _____ Type of government _____

Date of independence _____ From _____

Chief of state _____

Head of government _____

Name for citizen (e.g., Canadian) _____

Current population _____ World rank in population _____

Life expectancy _____ men _____ women Literacy _____ % male _____ % female

Ethnic groups _____

Major religions _____

Major languages _____

Land area _____ Water area _____ World rank in area _____

Five largest cities and their populations _____

_____

Bordering nations _____

_____

Climate _____

Terrain _____

Highest point and its elevation _____

Lowest point and its elevation _____

GDP _____ Per capita GDP _____ World rank in GDP _____

Major natural resources _____

Major industries _____

Chief agricultural products _____

Major exports _____

Major imports _____

East Timor

Gather these facts about East Timor, filling in the blanks.

Capital _____ Type of government _____

Date of independence _____ From _____

Chief of state _____

Head of government _____

Name for citizen (e.g., Canadian) _____

Current population _____ World rank in population _____

Life expectancy _____ men _____ women Literacy _____ % male _____ % female

Ethnic groups _____

Major religions _____

Major languages _____

Land area _____ Water area _____ World rank in area _____

Five largest cities and their populations _____

_____

Bordering nations _____

_____

Climate _____

Terrain _____

Highest point and its elevation _____

Lowest point and its elevation _____

GDP _____ Per capita GDP _____ World rank in GDP _____

Major natural resources _____

Major industries _____

Chief agricultural products _____

Major exports _____

Major imports _____

Indonesia

Gather these facts about Indonesia, filling in the blanks.

Capital _____ Type of government _____

Date of independence _____ From _____

Chief of state _____

Head of government _____

Name for citizen (e.g., Canadian) _____

Current population _____ World rank in population _____

Life expectancy _____ men _____ women   Literacy _____ % male _____ % female

Ethnic groups _____

Major religions _____

Major languages _____

Land area _____ Water area _____ World rank in area _____

Five largest cities and their populations _____

_____

Bordering nations _____

_____

Climate _____

Terrain _____

Highest point and its elevation _____

Lowest point and its elevation _____

GDP _____ Per capita GDP _____ World rank in GDP _____

Major natural resources _____

Major industries _____

Chief agricultural products _____

Major exports _____

Major imports _____

Malaysia

Gather these facts about Malaysia, filling in the blanks.

Capital _____ Type of government _____

Date of independence _____ From _____

Chief of state _____

Head of government _____

Name for citizen (e.g., Canadian) _____

Current population _____ World rank in population _____

Life expectancy _____ men _____ women   Literacy _____ % male _____ % female

Ethnic groups _____

Major religions _____

Major languages _____

Land area _____ Water area _____ World rank in area _____

Five largest cities and their populations _____

_____

Bordering nations _____

_____

Climate _____

Terrain _____

Highest point and its elevation _____

Lowest point and its elevation _____

GDP _____ Per capita GDP _____ World rank in GDP _____

Major natural resources _____

Major industries _____

Chief agricultural products _____

Major exports _____

Major imports _____

Philippines

Gather these facts about the Philippines, filling in the blanks.

Capital _____ Type of government _____

Date of independence _____ From _____

Chief of state _____

Head of government _____

Name for citizen (e.g., Canadian) _____

Current population _____ World rank in population _____

Life expectancy _____ men _____ women Literacy _____ % male _____ % female

Ethnic groups _____

Major religions _____

Major languages _____

Land area _____ Water area _____ World rank in area _____

Five largest cities and their populations _____

_____

Bordering nations _____

_____

Climate _____

Terrain _____

Highest point and its elevation _____

Lowest point and its elevation _____

GDP _____ Per capita GDP _____ World rank in GDP _____

Major natural resources _____

Major industries _____

Chief agricultural products _____

Major exports _____

Major imports _____

Singapore

Gather these facts about Singapore, filling in the blanks.

Capital _____ Type of government _____

Date of independence _____ From _____

Chief of state _____

Head of government _____

Name for citizen (e.g., Canadian) _____

Current population _____ World rank in population _____

Life expectancy _____ men _____ women   Literacy _____ % male _____ % female

Ethnic groups _____

Major religions _____

Major languages _____

Land area _____ Water area _____ World rank in area _____

Five largest cities and their populations _____

_____

Bordering nations _____

_____

Climate _____

Terrain _____

Highest point and its elevation _____

Lowest point and its elevation _____

GDP _____ Per capita GDP _____ World rank in GDP _____

Major natural resources _____

Major industries _____

Chief agricultural products _____

Major exports _____

Major imports _____

Australasia & Oceania

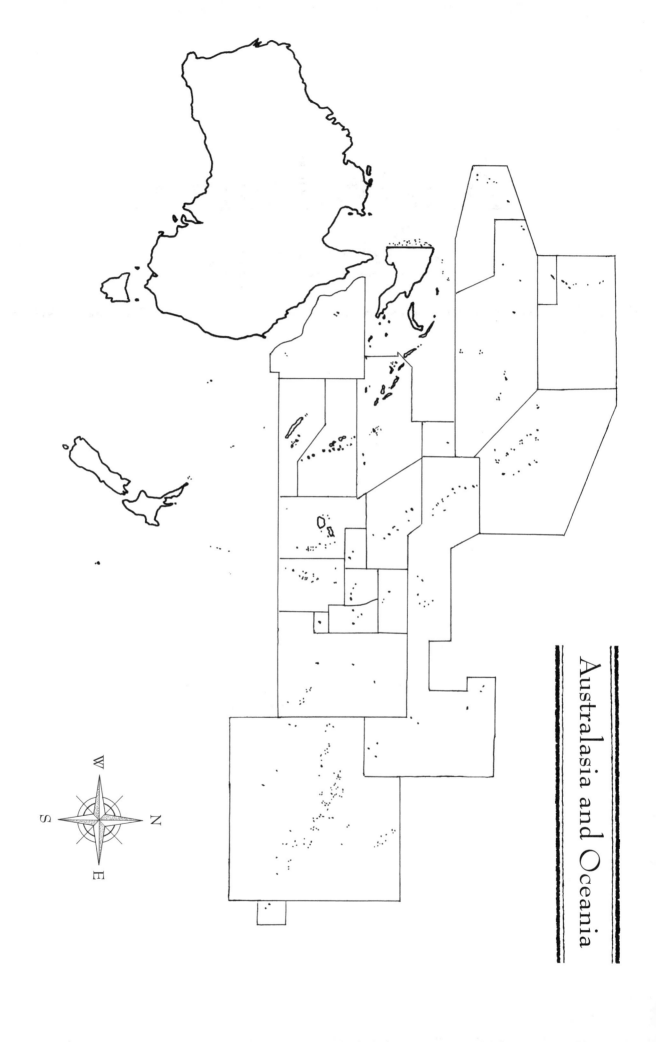

Australasia and Oceania

Australasia and Oceania

Gather these facts about the continent of Australasia and Oceania, filling in the blanks.

Total land area _____ Rank in area _____ of 7

Total population _____ Rank in population _____ of 7

Major languages _____

Major religions _____

Major natural resources _____

Longest river _____

Highest mountain _____

Lowest point (including ocean trenches) _____

Largest lake _____

Biggest desert _____

Biggest island _____

Three largest cities _____

Number of independent countries _____

Largest country _____

Smallest country _____

Most populous country _____

Least populous country _____

Most densely populated country _____

Least densely populated country _____

Largest dependent territory _____

Smallest dependent territory _____

Most populous dependent territory _____

Map It!

On the political map of Australasia and Oceania, label each independent country and its capital. Then use colored pencils to make each country a different color than the countries that border it.

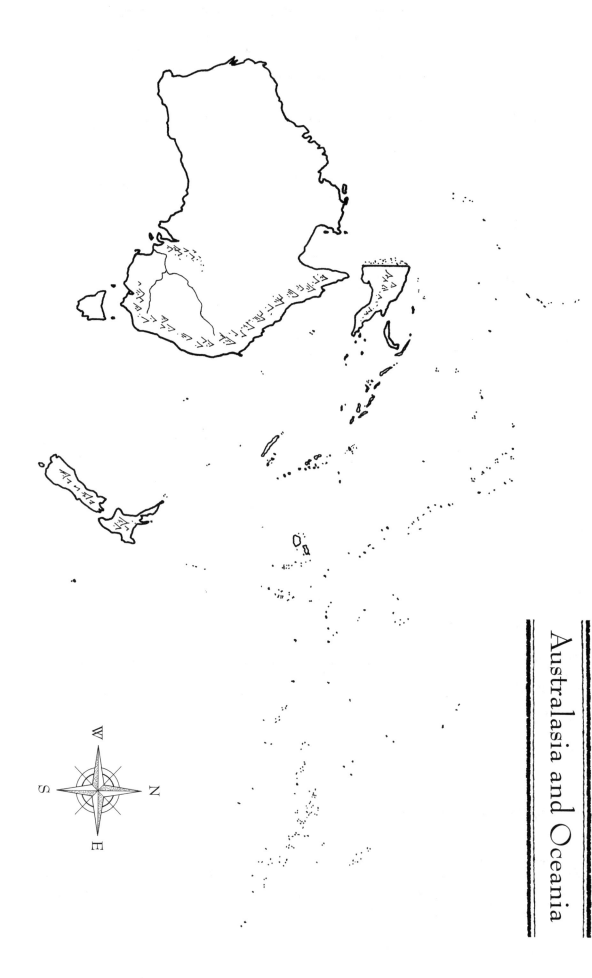

Australasia and Oceania

Map It!

Use this worksheet to organize your information as you research the following geographical features of Australasia and Oceania. This will help you be aware of the locations of all the items you will map before you actually begin so that you can use the space well. Finally, mark each item on the physical map of the continent.

The continent's major landforms (e.g., mountain ranges, plains, plateaus) _____

_____

_____

_____

The continent's major rivers and river basins _____

_____

_____

_____

The continent's major inland bodies of water _____

_____

_____

The continent's deserts _____

_____

_____

The continent's major islands, peninsulas, and capes _____

_____

_____

Bodies of water that border the continent _____

_____

_____

The continent's highest and lowest points and their elevations _____

_____

Any of the following lines of latitude that intersect the continent: Arctic Circle, Tropic of Cancer, Equator, Tropic of Capricorn, Antarctic Circle _____

_____

Any other special geographical features _____

_____

_____

Australia

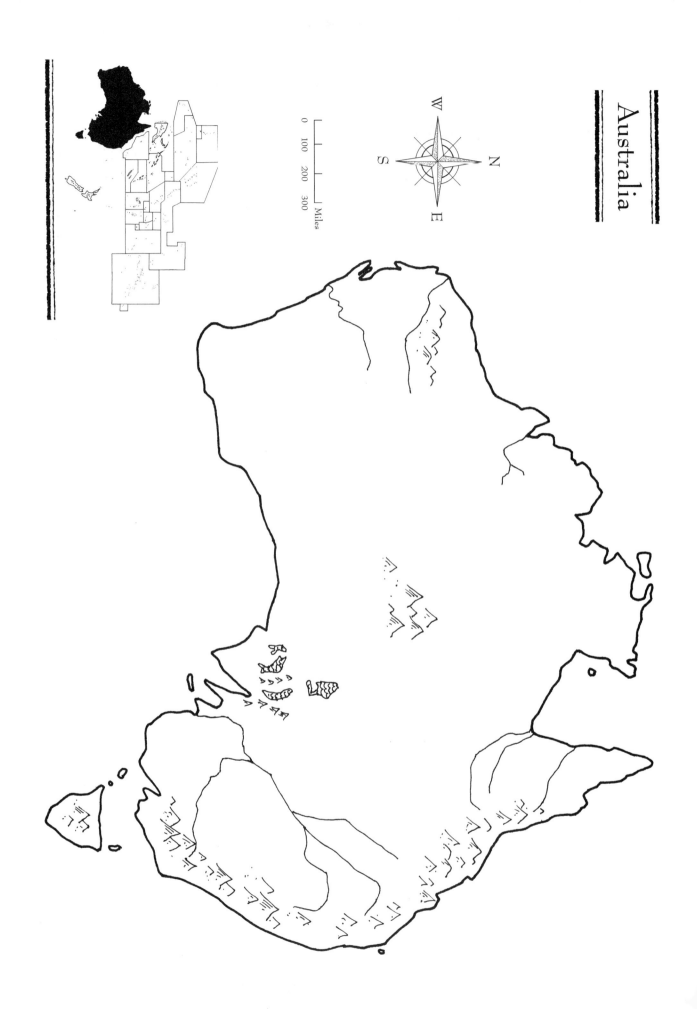

Map It!

Use this worksheet to organize your information as you research the following geographical features of Australia. This will help you be aware of the locations of all the items you will map before you actually begin so that you can use the space well. If Australia doesn't have one of the features listed, simply write "none" on the blank line. Finally, mark each item on the map of the country.

Australia's capital city _____

Australia's five largest cities _____

_____

Australia's major landforms (e.g., mountain ranges, plains, plateaus) _____

_____

_____

_____

Australia's highest and lowest points and their elevations _____

_____

Australia's major rivers and river basins _____

_____

_____

_____

Australia's major inland bodies of water _____

_____

_____

Australia's deserts _____

_____

Australia's important islands, peninsulas, and capes _____

_____

_____

Bodies of water that border Australia _____

_____

_____

Any other special geographical features _____

_____

Australia

Gather these facts about Australia, filling in the blanks.

Capital _____ Type of government _____

Date of independence _____ From _____

Chief of state _____

Head of government _____

Name for citizen (e.g., Canadian) _____

Current population _____ World rank in population _____

Life expectancy _____ men _____ women Literacy _____ % male _____ % female

Ethnic groups _____

Major religions _____

Major languages _____

Land area _____ Water area _____ World rank in area _____

Five largest cities and their populations _____

_____

Bordering nations _____

_____

Climate _____

Terrain _____

Highest point and its elevation _____

Lowest point and its elevation _____

GDP _____ Per capita GDP _____ World rank in GDP _____

Major natural resources _____

Major industries _____

Chief agricultural products _____

Major exports _____

Major imports _____

New Zealand

Map It!

Use this worksheet to organize your information as you research the following geographical features of New Zealand. This will help you be aware of the locations of all the items you will map before you actually begin so that you can use the space well. If New Zealand doesn't have one of the features listed, simply write "none" on the blank line. Finally, mark each item on the map of the country.

New Zealand's capital city _____

New Zealand's five largest cities _____

_____

New Zealand's major landforms (e.g., mountain ranges, plains, plateaus) _____

_____

_____

_____

New Zealand's highest and lowest points and their elevations _____

_____

New Zealand's major rivers and river basins _____

_____

_____

_____

New Zealand's major inland bodies of water _____

_____

_____

New Zealand's deserts _____

_____

New Zealand's important islands, peninsulas, and capes _____

_____

_____

Bodies of water that border New Zealand _____

_____

_____

Any other special geographical features _____

_____

New Zealand

Gather these facts about New Zealand, filling in the blanks.

Capital _____ Type of government _____

Date of independence _____ From _____

Chief of state _____

Head of government _____

Name for citizen (e.g., Canadian) _____

Current population _____ World rank in population _____

Life expectancy _____ men _____ women Literacy _____ % male _____ % female

Ethnic groups _____

Major religions _____

Major languages _____

Land area _____ Water area _____ World rank in area _____

Five largest cities and their populations _____

_____

Bordering nations _____

_____

Climate _____

Terrain _____

Highest point and its elevation _____

Lowest point and its elevation _____

GDP _____ Per capita GDP _____ World rank in GDP _____

Major natural resources _____

Major industries _____

Chief agricultural products _____

Major exports _____

Major imports _____

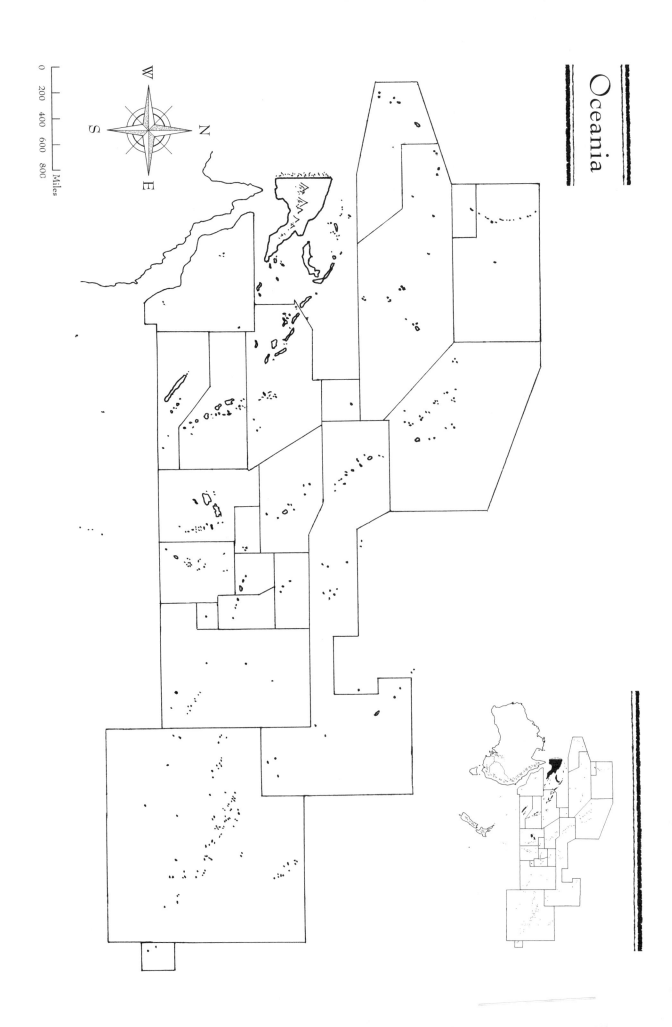

Oceania

Map It!

Use this worksheet to organize your information as you research the following geographical features of Oceania. This will help you be aware of the locations of all the items you will map before you actually begin so that you can use the space well. If the region doesn't have one of the features listed, simply write "none" on the blank line. Finally, mark each item on the map of the region.

The name of each independent country and its capital city _____

_____

_____

_____

_____

_____

_____

The region's major landforms (e.g., mountain ranges, plains, plateaus) _____

_____

_____

_____

The region's major rivers and river basins _____

_____

_____

_____

The region's major inland bodies of water _____

_____

_____

The region's deserts _____

_____

The region's important islands, peninsulas, and capes _____

_____

_____

Bodies of water that border the region _____

_____

_____

Any other special geographical features _____

_____

Fiji

Gather these facts about Fiji, filling in the blanks.

Capital _____ Type of government _____

Date of independence _____ From _____

Chief of state _____

Head of government _____

Name for citizen (e.g., Canadian) _____

Current population _____ World rank in population _____

Life expectancy _____ men _____ women   Literacy _____ % male _____ % female

Ethnic groups _____

Major religions _____

Major languages _____

Land area _____ Water area _____ World rank in area _____

Five largest cities and their populations _____

_____

Bordering nations _____

_____

Climate _____

Terrain _____

Highest point and its elevation _____

Lowest point and its elevation _____

GDP _____ Per capita GDP _____ World rank in GDP _____

Major natural resources _____

Major industries _____

Chief agricultural products _____

Major exports _____

Major imports _____

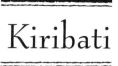

Kiribati

Gather these facts about Kiribati, filling in the blanks.

Capital _____ Type of government _____

Date of independence _____ From _____

Chief of state _____

Head of government _____

Name for citizen (e.g., Canadian) _____

Current population _____ World rank in population _____

Life expectancy _____ men _____ women Literacy _____ % male _____ % female

Ethnic groups _____

Major religions _____

Major languages _____

Land area _____ Water area _____ World rank in area _____

Five largest cities and their populations _____

_____

Bordering nations _____

_____

Climate _____

Terrain _____

Highest point and its elevation _____

Lowest point and its elevation _____

GDP _____ Per capita GDP _____ World rank in GDP _____

Major natural resources _____

Major industries _____

Chief agricultural products _____

Major exports _____

Major imports _____

Marshall Islands

Gather these facts about the Marshall Islands, filling in the blanks.

Capital _____ Type of government _____

Date of independence _____ From _____

Chief of state _____

Head of government _____

Name for citizen (e.g., Canadian) _____

Current population _____ World rank in population _____

Life expectancy _____ men _____ women   Literacy _____ % male _____ % female

Ethnic groups _____

Major religions _____

Major languages _____

Land area _____ Water area _____ World rank in area _____

Five largest cities and their populations _____

_____

Bordering nations _____

_____

Climate _____

Terrain _____

Highest point and its elevation _____

Lowest point and its elevation _____

GDP _____ Per capita GDP _____ World rank in GDP _____

Major natural resources _____

Major industries _____

Chief agricultural products _____

Major exports _____

Major imports _____

Micronesia

Gather these facts about the Federated States of Micronesia, filling in the blanks.

Capital _____ _____ Type of government _____

Date of independence _____ From _____ _____

Chief of state _____

Head of government _____

Name for citizen (e.g., Canadian) _____

Current population _____ World rank in population _____

Life expectancy _____ men _____ women Literacy _____ % male _____ % female

Ethnic groups _____

Major religions _____

Major languages _____

Land area _____ Water area _____ World rank in area _____

Five largest cities and their populations _____

_____

Bordering nations _____

_____

Climate _____

Terrain _____

Highest point and its elevation _____

Lowest point and its elevation _____

GDP _____ Per capita GDP _____ World rank in GDP _____

Major natural resources _____

Major industries _____

Chief agricultural products _____

Major exports _____

Major imports _____

Nauru

Gather these facts about Nauru, filling in the blanks.

Capital _____ Type of government _____

Date of independence _____ From _____

Chief of state _____

Head of government _____

Name for citizen (e.g., Canadian) _____

Current population _____ World rank in population _____

Life expectancy _____ men _____ women   Literacy _____ % male _____ % female

Ethnic groups _____

Major religions _____

Major languages _____

Land area _____ Water area _____ World rank in area _____

Five largest cities and their populations _____

_____

Bordering nations _____

_____

Climate _____

Terrain _____

Highest point and its elevation _____

Lowest point and its elevation _____

GDP _____ Per capita GDP _____ World rank in GDP _____

Major natural resources _____

Major industries _____

Chief agricultural products _____

Major exports _____

Major imports _____

Palau

Gather these facts about Palau, filling in the blanks.

Capital _____ Type of government _____

Date of independence _____ From _____

Chief of state _____

Head of government _____

Name for citizen (e.g., Canadian) _____

Current population _____ World rank in population _____

Life expectancy _____ men _____ women   Literacy _____ % male _____ % female

Ethnic groups _____

Major religions _____

Major languages _____

Land area _____ Water area _____ World rank in area _____

Five largest cities and their populations _____

_____

Bordering nations _____

_____

Climate _____

Terrain _____

Highest point and its elevation _____

Lowest point and its elevation _____

GDP _____ Per capita GDP _____ World rank in GDP _____

Major natural resources _____

Major industries _____

Chief agricultural products _____

Major exports _____

Major imports _____

Papua New Guinea

Gather these facts about Papua New Guinea, filling in the blanks.

Capital _____ Type of government _____

Date of independence _____ From _____

Chief of state _____

Head of government _____

Name for citizen (e.g., Canadian) _____

Current population _____ World rank in population _____

Life expectancy _____ men _____ women   Literacy _____ % male _____ % female

Ethnic groups _____

Major religions _____

Major languages _____

Land area _____ Water area _____ World rank in area _____

Five largest cities and their populations _____

_____

Bordering nations _____

_____

Climate _____

Terrain _____

Highest point and its elevation _____

Lowest point and its elevation _____

GDP _____ Per capita GDP _____ World rank in GDP _____

Major natural resources _____

Major industries _____

Chief agricultural products _____

Major exports _____

Major imports _____

Samoa

Gather these facts about Samoa, filling in the blanks.

Capital _____ Type of government _____

Date of independence _____ From _____

Chief of state _____

Head of government _____

Name for citizen (e.g., Canadian) _____

Current population _____ World rank in population _____

Life expectancy _____ men _____ women Literacy _____ % male _____ % female

Ethnic groups _____

Major religions _____

Major languages _____

Land area _____ Water area _____ World rank in area _____

Five largest cities and their populations _____

_____

Bordering nations _____

_____

Climate _____

Terrain _____

Highest point and its elevation _____

Lowest point and its elevation _____

GDP _____ Per capita GDP _____ World rank in GDP _____

Major natural resources _____

Major industries _____

Chief agricultural products _____

Major exports _____

Major imports _____

Solomon Islands

Gather these facts about the Solomon Islands, filling in the blanks.

Capital _____ Type of government _____

Date of independence _____ From _____

Chief of state _____

Head of government _____

Name for citizen (e.g., Canadian) _____

Current population _____ World rank in population _____

Life expectancy _____ men _____ women Literacy _____ % male _____ % female

Ethnic groups _____

Major religions _____

Major languages _____

Land area _____ Water area _____ World rank in area _____

Five largest cities and their populations _____

_____

Bordering nations _____

_____

Climate _____

Terrain _____

Highest point and its elevation _____

Lowest point and its elevation _____

GDP _____ Per capita GDP _____ World rank in GDP _____

Major natural resources _____

Major industries _____

Chief agricultural products _____

Major exports _____

Major imports _____

Tonga

Gather these facts about Tonga, filling in the blanks.

Capital _____ Type of government _____

Date of independence _____ From _____

Chief of state _____

Head of government _____

Name for citizen (e.g., Canadian) _____

Current population _____ World rank in population _____

Life expectancy _____ men _____ women Literacy _____ % male _____ % female

Ethnic groups _____

Major religions _____

Major languages _____

Land area _____ Water area _____ World rank in area _____

Five largest cities and their populations _____

_____

Bordering nations _____

_____

Climate _____

Terrain _____

Highest point and its elevation _____

Lowest point and its elevation _____

GDP _____ Per capita GDP _____ World rank in GDP _____

Major natural resources _____

Major industries _____

Chief agricultural products _____

Major exports _____

Major imports _____

Tuvalu

Gather these facts about Tuvalu, filling in the blanks.

Capital _____ Type of government _____

Date of independence _____ From _____

Chief of state _____

Head of government _____

Name for citizen (e.g., Canadian) _____

Current population _____ World rank in population _____

Life expectancy _____ men _____ women   Literacy _____ % male _____ % female

Ethnic groups _____

Major religions _____

Major languages _____

Land area _____ Water area _____ World rank in area _____

Five largest cities and their populations _____

_____

Bordering nations _____

_____

Climate _____

Terrain _____

Highest point and its elevation _____

Lowest point and its elevation _____

GDP _____ Per capita GDP _____ World rank in GDP _____

Major natural resources _____

Major industries _____

Chief agricultural products _____

Major exports _____

Major imports _____

Vanuatu

Gather these facts about Vanuatu, filling in the blanks.

Capital _____ Type of government _____

Date of independence _____ From _____

Chief of state _____

Head of government _____

Name for citizen (e.g., Canadian) _____

Current population _____ World rank in population _____

Life expectancy _____ men _____ women Literacy _____ % male _____ % female

Ethnic groups _____

Major religions _____

Major languages _____

Land area _____ Water area _____ World rank in area _____

Five largest cities and their populations _____

_____

Bordering nations _____

_____

Climate _____

Terrain _____

Highest point and its elevation _____

Lowest point and its elevation _____

GDP _____ Per capita GDP _____ World rank in GDP _____

Major natural resources _____

Major industries _____

Chief agricultural products _____

Major exports _____

Major imports _____

Antarctica &
the Arctic

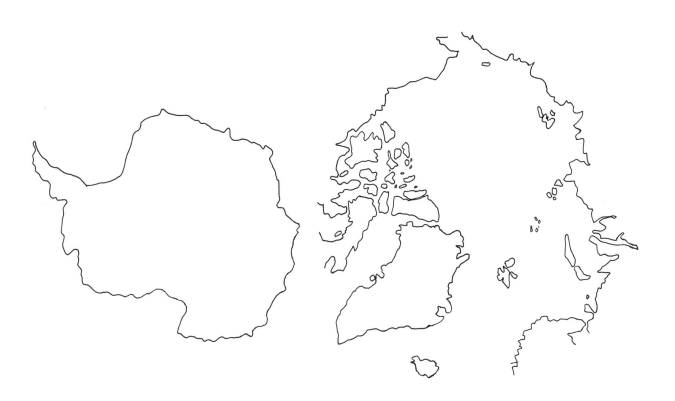

Antarctica

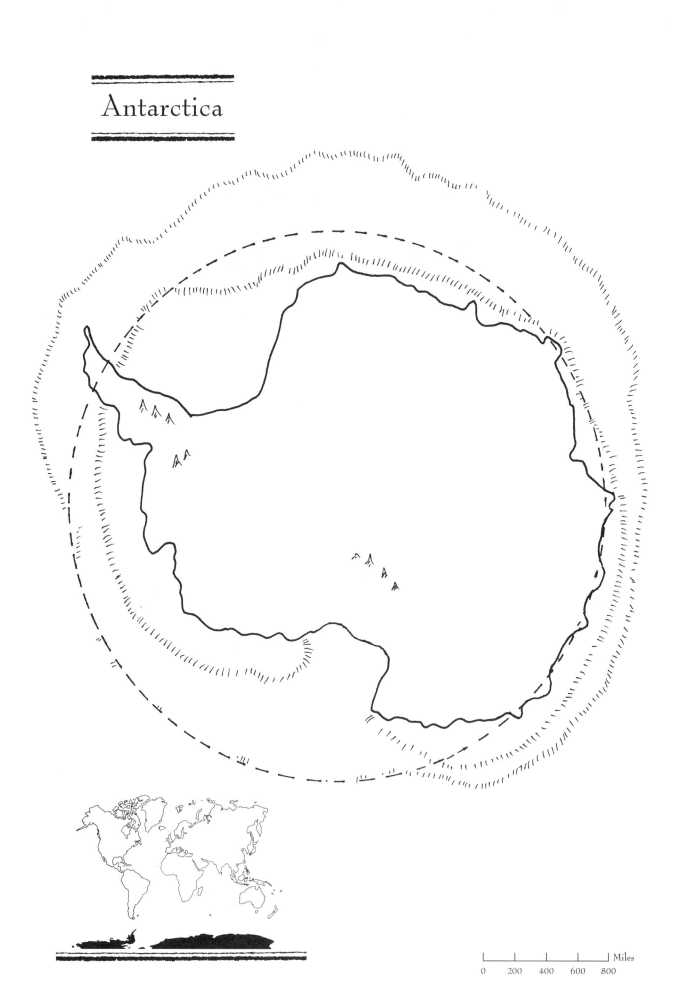

Miles

0   200   400   600   800

Map It!

Use this worksheet to organize your information as you research the following geographical features of Antarctica. This will help you be aware of the locations of all the items you will map before you actually begin so that you can use the space well. Finally, mark each item on the map of the continent.

Antarctica's major landforms (e.g., mountain ranges, plains, plateaus) _____

_____

_____

_____

Antarctica's major ice shelves _____

_____

_____

_____

Antarctica's major islands, peninsulas, and capes _____

_____

_____

Bodies of water that border Antarctica _____

_____

_____

Antarctica's highest and lowest points and their elevations _____

_____

Antarctica's major subglacial lakes _____

_____

_____

Antarctica's deserts _____

_____

Antarctica's rivers _____

_____

On your map, also indicate

- Greater and Lesser Antarctica (also called Eastern and Western Antarctica)
- The Antarctic Circle
- The South Pole
- The extent of winter pack ice and summer pack ice

Antarctica

Gather these facts about the continent of Antarctica, filling in the blanks.

What does the name *Antarctica* mean? _____ _____

What did the ancients call Antarctica, and why did they think it existed even though it hadn't been discovered yet? _____

_____

What year was the first confirmed sighting of Antarctica? _____

When was it established that Antarctica is a continent and not just a group of islands? _____

Antarctica's total land area _____ Rank in area _____ of 7

Percentage of Antarctica covered in ice _____ Average thickness of the ice _____

_____ % of the earth's ice and _____ % of the earth's fresh water is found in Antarctica.

How many people live in Antarctica during the winter and how many during the summer? What kind of work do most of these people do? _____

_____

What natural resources are found in Antarctica? _____

_____

What industries make up Antarctica's economic activity? _____

_____

What is the purpose of the Antarctic Treaty System? How many nations participate? In summary, what do these nations agree to? _____

_____

_____

_____

Which nations have made territorial claims in Antarctica? Are these claims recognized by other countries? Which nations have reserved the right to make claims in the future? _____

_____

_____

_____

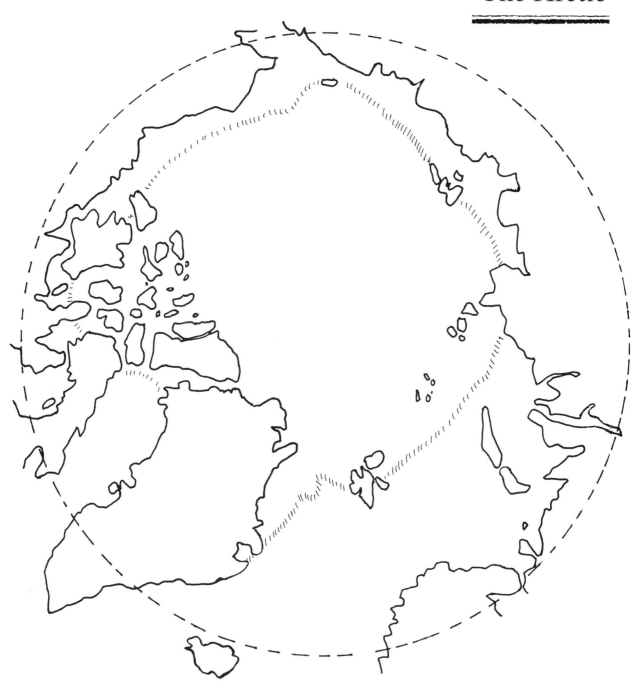

The Arctic

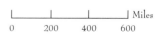

Miles

0   200   400   600

Map It!

Use this worksheet to organize your information as you research the following geographical features of the Arctic. This will help you be aware of the locations of all the items you will map before you actually begin so that you can use the space well. Finally, mark each item on the map of the Arctic.

The continents that extend into the Arctic _____ _____

_____

The countries of the Arctic _____

_____

_____

The Arctic's major islands and island groupings _____

_____

_____

_____

_____

The Arctic's major landforms (e.g., mountain ranges, plains, plateaus) _____

_____

_____

_____

_____

The Arctic's major bodies of water _____

_____

_____

_____

_____

The most northerly inhabited place in the world _____

_____

The world's northernmost town _____

The world's northernmost city _____

On your map, also indicate

- The Arctic Circle
- The North Pole
- The extent of summer pack ice

The Arctic

Gather these facts about the Arctic, filling in the blanks.

Describe two different criteria for defining the Arctic region. _____

_____

_____

_____

Define the Arctic Circle. _____

_____

Define the North Pole. _____

_____

Describe the climate of the Arctic. _____

_____

_____

What natural resources are found in the Arctic? _____

_____

_____

What are the midnight sun and polar night? How are they different at the Arctic Circle and the North Pole? _____

_____

_____

What is the approximate population of the Arctic? _____

What are the names of the primary Arctic peoples? _____

_____

_____

Describe the traditional lifestyle of the Arctic peoples. _____

_____

_____

_____

_____

Who were the first European explorers of the Arctic? _____

Appendices

Appendix A

Additional Mapping Activities

In addition to the world mapping activities on pages 11 and 13, students can use the blank maps of the world to mark many different places, trends, and events. Even if a student is using *Maps of the World* as a workbook, we suggest that you photocopy the world maps on pages 10 and 12 before they are used so that the student can undertake more than one activity. You may also want to photocopy the maps of the continents in case you'd like to adapt any of these activities to those larger-scale maps.

Note that two mapping activities can be done on the same map to show the relationship between them, for example, the relationship between the world's geography and the distribution of natural resources, industries, and agricultural products. Alternatively, duplicates of the same map can be used to plot different themes, for example, gross domestic product per capita and literacy rates, and students can be asked to make observations about what the maps suggest when looked at together.

The online version of *The World Factbook* (https://www.cia.gov/cia/publications/factbook/index .html) is a good source of data for thematic maps. It provides handy tables that rank the world's nations according to many themes, including area, population, life expectancy, literacy, and gross domestic product. To link to a table, select Guide to Rank Order Pages or look for the "Rank Order" bar graph symbol beside these entries in the nation profiles. Refer to Appendix E for other helpful resources.

Activities

- Identify which ten countries have the world's largest populations and which ten have the world's smallest populations. Create a two-color key, using one color for the largest populations and one color for the smallest populations. On the world political map, color the twenty countries that you identified the appropriate color according to your key.

- Make or find a table showing each country and its population density. Using different colors for different ranges, create a key for population density. On the world political map, follow your key to color the countries the appropriate color. (For example, your ranges might be less than 1 person per square mile, 1–15, 16–30, 31–60, 61–130, 131–260, 261–500, over 500.)

  Note: Activities similar to the two above can be undertaken for virtually any theme for which a student can find data. The possibilities range from life expectancy, literacy rates, and GDP per capita to world religions, HIV/AIDS prevalence rates, and oil consumption and production.

- Gather information about the major natural resources, industries, and agricultural products of each of the world's continents. Construct a key that represents them (e.g., a tree for timber or sunglasses for tourism). Label the world outline map accordingly.

- Identify the countries of the world in which armed conflicts are currently underway. Shade those countries on the world political map.

  Note: Older students can do further research and make a more detailed map, creating a key to show other nations involved in the conflicts and factors such as the type of conflict and its duration.

- Identify the twenty five cities in the world with the largest populations. Create a key by assigning a different symbol to each range of five. Plot the cities on the world political map using the appropriate symbol.

  Note: Alternatively, or in addition for comparison, students can identify the twenty-five cities in the world with the largest urban-area populations, sometimes called the largest metropolitan areas. These two lists have some overlap but are quite different.

Appendix B

Student Explorations

These diverse activities provide students of different ages and different learning styles with a forum to delve deeper into learning about the world's nations. The activities require varying amounts of research and can be made more or less comprehensive at your discretion. Where necessary, you can alter the directions, give additional instructions, or provide specific ideas for the particular nation being studied. Choose the activities that are best suited to your student or students.

As you select activities, consider the possibility of planning a culminating event during which each student can express his or her newly acquired knowledge. The event can be as simple as inviting the class next door (or the homeschooled children down the street) to come hear poems and stories and view your students' written work. Conversely, the event could be as involved as hosting a parent/neighborhood dinner or a homeschool group event featuring food, songs, games, stories, oral presentations, and plays. For example, you might sponsor a "Passport Night," with passports that can be stamped as a visitor learns something from the displays and presentations about each country represented. No matter how simple or elaborate the culminating event is, many teachers find it useful to have a broad outline in mind before assigning these student explorations and other activities.

- Make a topographical model of the country using dough, clay, or papier-mâché. Form and label the nation's major rivers and bodies of water, mountain ranges, plains, deserts, and other geographical characteristics. In addition, label the nation's capital, the nation's five largest cities, and three other important sites of your choice. Note that *The Stuff That Fun Is Made Of* by Selena LaPorte has an excellent collection of easy recipes and instructions for making homemade doughs and paints for landscape and relief maps, including those for making the base, water, mountains, deserts and plains, and even volcanoes. See Appendix E.

- Research and plan a route for visiting key places in the nation. First identify significant places that you would want to see if you were to tour the nation. Plot these on a map. Then plan your route and determine how you would get from place to place. You might want to study a travel guide to help you. Alternatively, you could do the same thing for a city in the nation.

- Find a picture of the nation's flag in a book or online. Research the symbolism behind the flag's design. Then draw or paint a picture of the flag and write a paragraph explaining what the different elements of the design represent.

- Create a collage about the nation. From old newspapers and magazines, cut out words, letters, and pictures that relate to the nation's people, history, geography, economy, and current events. Plan your design and then glue the cutouts to a large piece of paper so that it is completely covered. Be sure to include the nation's name.

- Create a postcard. Illustrate the front with a scene that you think represents the nation well. On the back write home as if you were visiting the nation. Explain the significance of the picture, and share several interesting facts you've learned or experiences you've had on your imaginary trip.

- Research the types of foods grown and prepared in the nation. Use the Internet or your library to find recipes, and prepare a typical meal that people in this country might eat.

- Make a brochure or poster encouraging people to visit the country, such as might be produced by that nation's tourism industry or government to persuade people to come as tourists. Include interesting facts and descriptions of the nation's people, history, geography, climate, and economy that might entice others to visit. Be sure to include both pictures and words and use lots of color.

- Write a travel advisory bulletin for the nation, such as those put out by the U.S. government. Unlike a travel brochure or poster, the purpose of your bulletin is to protect and inform citizens of your own nation who are considering traveling there. Consider these questions as you draft your bulletin: What factors do people need to take into account as they decide whether to visit this nation? Are there any issues of safety, such as illness, violence, or natural disasters? If they decide to visit, what do people need to know? Do they need any special paperwork to enter the country? What kind of conditions and climate should they be prepared for? Where is your nation's embassy located if travelers need help while visiting? (See http://travel.state.gov/travel/cis_pa_tw/cis/cis_1765.html)

  Note: For those nations where travel includes special risk, it might be interesting for a student or a team of students to produce both a travel brochure or poster and a travel advisory bulletin. They could then discuss the different reasons people travel to that nation in spite of the risks and whether they agree that those purposes are worth it.

- Write and illustrate a picture book that introduces younger children to the nation. What essential facts should they know? What about the nation will catch their interest? What makes the nation unique? What would they like to see illustrated? Be sure to include a front and back cover. When your book is done, read it to a younger child.

- Write and illustrate a picture book about a famous person from the nation whom you find very interesting. What interests you about this person? Is there something unique about him or her? What is this person famous for? What has he or she contributed and achieved? Has being from this nation made a difference in this person's life or a difference for the nation? Ask yourself questions like these and then tell the person's story in your own words and with your own illustrations. Be sure to make a front and back cover for your book. When your book is done, read it aloud to others.

- Make a historical timeline for the nation on a long sheet of paper or by joining several smaller sheets together. Include the lives and accomplishments of some of the nation's famous citizens as well as major events in its history, such as its date of independence. Include a few current events to bring your timeline to the present. To put things in perspective, add three or four major world events as well as the lives of a few key historical figures from outside the nation.

- Pick a key event in the nation's history that you think makes a good story and write a skit or play about it. Act it out for a live audience or create a video production.

- Write a newspaper article about a key event in the nation, either historical or current. For a larger project or for a group project, create a whole newspaper about key events in the nation's past and present day. Include a human-interest feature profiling a famous citizen or one of the nation's people groups. Begin by studying a real newspaper to see how articles are composed.

- Write a report about the nation, focusing on life in the nation today. Include information about the nation's people and culture, geography, climate, animal and plant life, and economy. Be sure to include good descriptions and interesting facts so that your readers will learn what makes this nation unique.

- Imagine you are a citizen of this country today. First decide who you are (e.g., child or adult, man or woman, city dweller or villager, your occupation), and research how this person would live. Then write a series of journal entries that show what daily life is like for you. Include descriptions of your surroundings so that others can envision your life.

- Write a travel essay about the nation or one of its important cities. First read examples of travel writing. (These kinds of creative essays can be found in magazines, books of essays, and the travel sections of newspapers.) Then research the nation or city and re-create a trip in writing, with descriptions of what you saw, who you met, what you ate, and how you traveled. Think about all your senses. What did you see, hear, smell, feel, and taste? You may want to focus on one interesting city, or you might want to lead your readers on a tour of the nation's different regions or famous places. If you really have visited the nation, that's great, but your trip can be imaginary.

- Interview someone who has lived in this nation and, using stories, facts, and quotations from your interview, write a creative essay that shares the person's experiences and thoughts about life in this nation. First work with an adult to arrange the interview. The interview could be in person, on the phone, over email, or through the mail. Then read examples of published character sketches. (These kinds of creative essays can be found in magazines, newspaper features, and books of essays.) Next, prepare your list of questions, being sure to include a variety of topics. Depending on what you've arranged, send your questions to the person or refer to the list during your conversation. If the interview is in person, request permission to record it to help you in your writing.

- Prepare and give an oral presentation on one of the world's dependent entities. Find out about its people, geography, and economy. How is the territory or commonwealth governed? What rights and responsibilities does it share with the nation? What is different? Learn about its history before and after becoming associated with the nation and how the association began. Investigate how the relationship benefits each party and whether the relationship has been a detriment for either party in any way. Create visual aids, including a map that shows the location of the dependency and the location of the nation, to use in your presentation.

- Prepare and give an oral presentation about the extreme points of the earth, also called geographical superlatives. Make a poster or computer slide show to use in your presentation. Include a world map that pinpoints the locations you are discussing. Where possible, find photographs of these places; otherwise create your own representations.

Note: The worksheets on pages 11 and 13 guide students in identifying and mapping many of the geographical superlatives. That work can be the foundation for this project.

- Prepare and give an oral presentation about a famous explorer. How did this person's discoveries affect the content of maps drawn during that time? Make a map of the explorer's voyages or travels to use in your presentation.

Appendix C

Conceptual Social Studies Exercises

To complete these brief conceptual activities, students can write one or more paragraphs in response, present an oral report on one of the topics, or discuss the answers to one or more activities in a group context. Note that some activities may not be suited to all nations.

- Choose a nation. Name and locate two nations that are larger than this nation in area, two that are about the same size, and two that are smaller. Do the same for population.

- Calculate the nation's population density in people per square mile. How does it compare with surrounding nations' population densities?

- Compare the population of the nation to the total population of the world. Express this comparison as a percentage.

- Study a physical map of the nation. Where do you think most of the population would live? Why? Use a population map to test your hypothesis. Were you right or wrong? Explain.

- Research a natural disaster that the nation is prone to. How is this hazard related to the nation's geography? How do people protect themselves against it?

- Study a political world map printed twenty years ago and compare it to a current world map. What names have changed? Identify one country that now has a different name. What historical events led to this name change?

Appendix D

Vocabulary

This appendix gives ideas for studying terms related to geography and cartography. The terms range from the simple to the advanced. You may find it helpful to make a note of those terms you think are appropriate for your students. If they know the meaning of all but five of the terms, have them learn only those five. Conversely, if they are unfamiliar with most of the terms, choose a realistic number for each student to explore and learn. Students can use this list to

- Define and memorize the terms.

- Produce an individual or class reference book of terms. Assign each student a number of terms to write a definition for or, where possible, depict in a sketch. From this research, a book of definitions can be made, allotting one page for each definition. This book could be added to throughout the year. (Students may need a dictionary to help them with this activity.)

- Play reinforcement games such as *Go Fish* or *Concentration*. For example, write some terms from the list on index cards and have students take turns pairing them with definitions written on other index cards.

- Produce an individual or class collection of maps and illustrations that exemplify the cartography terms. Have students use books, newspapers, magazines, and the Internet to locate examples of political maps, topographic maps, different kinds of thematic maps, small- and large-scale maps, and different map projections. In addition, have students locate maps on which they can identify other cartography terms, such the parts of maps and terms related to latitude and longitude. Students can duplicate, cut out, or print the maps as appropriate, gather them into a book or notebook, and label them appropriately.

- Identify real-world locations that match the geographical feature terms. Have students use an atlas or other maps to locate good examples of terms such as *divide, isthmus, plateau,* and *tributary.*

- Create an imaginary landscape that demonstrates an understanding of the geographical feature terms. Have students make a map, draw a bird's-eye picture, or construct a topographical model of a landscape that includes the geographical features you specify. Be sure the landscape shows the defining characteristics of the terms.

Cartography

absolute location	conical projections	key	Prime Meridian
Antarctic Circle	country	large-scale map	relief map
Arctic Circle	cylindrical projections	latitude	scale
atlas	dependency	legend	small-scale map
azimuthal projections	elevation	longitude	South Pole
bird's-eye view	Equator	map	territory
border	exact location	map projections	thematic maps
boundary	globe	nation	title
cartographer	grid	North Pole	topographical map
cartography	hemisphere	physical map	Tropic of Cancer
compass	international date line	political map	Tropic of Capricorn

Geographical Features

archipelago	distributary	landmass	point
atoll	divide	locks	polar cap
basin	escarpment	lowlands	reef
bay	fault	mesa	river
breakwater	fjord	mountain peak	sea
canal	foothills	mountain range	sound
canyon	fork	oasis	spit
cape	glacier	ocean	strait
continent	gorge	ocean ridge	terrain
continental drift	harbor	ocean trench	tributary
continental plate	highlands	oceanic plate	valley
continental shelf	isthmus	peninsula	volcano
continental shield	lagoon	plain	waterfall
continental slope	lake	plate boundaries	
delta	landform	plateau	

Climate and Biomes

arctic	marsh	savannah	temperature
biomes	Mediterranean	steppe	treeline
broadleaf forests	mountain	subarctic	tropical and temperate
climate	coniferous forests	subtropical	grasslands
climatic zones	polar regions	swamp	tropical rain forests
cold desert	prairie	taiga	tropics
dry woodlands	precipitation	temperate rain forests	tundra
hot desert	rain shadow	temperate zones	wetlands

Human Geography

agriculture	exports	industries	purchasing power parity
birth rate	GDP per capita	infant mortality	religion
culture	globalism	language	services
death rate	goods	life expectancy	standard of living
developed world	gross domestic product	literacy	trade bloc
developing world	(GDP)	natural resources	
economy	imports	population density	

Resources

Many excellent resources are available for studying world geography. The resources listed here are just a sampling. They include books, Internet sites, subscription sites, and movies available through many libraries and schools. As with all material for your students, you will want to preview all of these sources yourself.

Books

These are just some of the many good books available. There may be some here that you'd like to add to your own list of favorites. Many series of books about individual countries are also available, including the Ticket to... series for grades 2–4 (Carolrhoda Books) and the Enchantment of the World series for grades 5–9 (Children's Press). Because multiple authors contribute to each series, the quality of books varies. You may want to research which series has the best book on the particular country your student is researching. Of course, new editions of atlases and other reference books are continually being published; your libraries and bookstores will have updated versions.

Janice VanCleave's Geography for Every Kid:
Easy Activities That Make Learning Geography Fun

Author: Janice Pratt VanCleave
Publication: New York: Wiley, 1993
ISBN: 0471598410
Description: 224 pages, ages 8–12

Summary: While *Geography for Every Kid* isn't graphically flashy like many other geography resources, it is rich in learning possibilities. A former science teacher, VanCleave is the author of more than twenty other science books for children. This book uses simple exercises and activities to introduce basic concepts of geography. Kids can construct a clay map, make a compass rose, plot the track of a hurricane, and more. Each activity is broken down into its purpose, a list of materials, step-by-step instructions, expected results, and an easy to understand explanation.

The Stuff That Fun Is Made Of:
A Comprehensive Collection of Recipes for Play and Learning

Author: Selena LaPorte
Publication: Lynnwood, Wash.: Emerald Books, 2001
ISBN: 188300277X
Description: 160 pages

Summary: *The Stuff That Fun Is Made Of* contains simple, inexpensive recipes and instructions for making homemade landscape and relief map doughs and paints. In addition, you'll find specific instructions for making blue-water dough, dough that's good for forming mountains, and a dough especially for deserts and plains. Students can form the shape of the country, fill in rivers and lakes, and build up mountain ranges, even volcanoes.

Maps and Mapping

Author: Deborah Chancellor
Publication: New York: Kingfisher, 2004
ISBN: 0753457598
Description: 47 pages, ages 5–8

Summary: With graphics-filled pages and short bursts of text, *Maps and Mapping* introduces different types of maps and helps children understand how they work. Students learn about compass points, map keys and scales, and colors and contours and discover how reading maps reveals information about both the natural and man-made world. Includes several projects, from making a compass to constructing a relief map.

Mapping the World

Author: Sylvia A. Johnson
Publication: New York: Atheneum Books, 1999
ISBN: 0689818130
Description: 32 pages, ages 9–12

Summary: With clear, well-organized text and intriguing full-color reproductions of historical maps, kids trace the history of mapmaking from Babylonian times until today. Johnson introduces early mapmakers and geographers and shows how maps both reflect and change people's view of the world. Not only is this a beautiful book, but the illustrations are well-integrated with the text so that kids are able to learn from the historical reproductions.

Mapping the World

Author: Walter Oleksy
Publication: New York: Franklin Watts, 2003
ISBN: 0531166368
Description: 63 pages, ages 10–12

Summary: This nonfiction chapter book introduces students to pioneering geographers and explorers who undertook painstaking study of the known world and brave exploration of the unknown world to create the first scientific maps. Aided by many color historical maps, photographs, and paintings, students survey the evolution of mapmaking from ancient times until today.

How Maps Are Made

Author: Martyn Bramwell
Illustrator: George Fryer
Publication: Minneapolis: Lerner Publications, 1998
ISBN: 0822529203
Description: 48 pages, ages 9–14

Summary: Part of the series Maps and Mapmakers, *How Maps Are Made* is an excellent resource that describes the methods and tools used to make maps and, more briefly, the history of mapmaking. Many pages include directions for activities that will help students understand and apply what they're learning about map projections, size, distance, scale, compasses, and more. Includes colorful photographs, illustrations, charts, and maps.

Small Worlds: Maps and Mapmaking

Author: Karen Romano Young
Publication: New York: Scholastic, 2002
ISBN: 043909545X
Description: 128 pages, age 12 and up

Summary: From its opening page, this book uses good storytelling, clear explanations, and helpful graphics to show how maps are put together, how to use a map to get oriented, and the use of hundreds of different kinds of maps. Includes the history and technical aspects of cartography, historical and modern real-life stories, and the practical use of maps that range from maps of the neighborhood to maps of space. This unique book is enjoyable and informative.

National Geographic Beginner's World Atlas

Author: National Geographic Society (U.S.)
Publication: Washington, D.C.: National Geographic Society, 2005
ISBN: 0792242114
Description: 64 pages, ages 5–8

Summary: This is a good first atlas. Large, easy-to-read physical and political maps introduce children to the world and each of its continents. Color photographs and simple text supplement the maps. Back matter includes a map keyed to a chart of geographic superlatives, a glossary, a pronunciation guide, and an index.

National Geographic World Atlas for Young Explorers

Author: National Geographic Society (U.S.)
Publication: Washington, D.C.: National Geographic Society, 2003
ISBN: 0792228790
Description: 192 pages, ages 8–12

Summary: Considered the best children's atlas by *School Library Journal* and highly recommended by many others, this award-winning atlas presents world, regional, and thematic maps as well as photographic essays on each continent. Locator globes and color coding help young readers find what they need and make easy comparisons, while fact boxes, charts, geographic superlatives, national flags, a glossary, and a detailed index further enhance the book's reference value and appeal.

The Usborne Internet-Linked Children's World Atlas

Author: Stephanie Turnbull and Emma Helbrough
Publication: Tulsa, Okla.: EDC Publishing, 2005
ISBN: 0794510795
Description: 144 pages, ages 9 and up

Summary: This compact-sized atlas has a stunningly beautiful presentation. Coverage of each continent includes a political overview map and introductory facts, arresting satellite images, photographs and descriptions of key sights, and several larger-scale political and environmental maps covering the continent up close. Internet use is not necessary, but the book contains descriptions of websites recommended for further exploration of topics discussed. While not the best atlas for reference use, it is great for browsing and piquing interest. Students of all ages will enjoy exploring this vivid view of our world.

National Geographic Student Atlas of the World

Author: National Geographic Society (U.S.)
Publication: Washington, D.C.: National Geographic Society, 2005
ISBN: 0792271688
Description: 144 pages, ages 12 and up

Summary: This atlas is designed to demonstrate basic geographic concepts and encourage students to compare and contrast information for different parts of the world. It is excellent for those purposes, but it may not contain all the information students need to create their own detailed political or physical maps. The *National Geographic World*

Atlas for Young Explorers provides greater detail, including more regional maps showing physical and political information, while this atlas reproduces whole continents several times to show different themes such as climate, precipitation, population, and economics. The physical and political maps are very readable, but quite basic. A strength of this atlas is the special "Focus on" section included for each continent, covering topics such as South America's Amazon Rain Forest and Australia's Great Barrier Reef. This atlas also includes a section on learning about maps and forty pages on the world as a whole, covering both physical and human aspects of world geography.

Dorling Kindersley World Atlas

Author: DK Publishing, Inc.
Publication: New York: DK Publishing, 2005
ISBN: 0756613752
Description: 354 pages, ages 14 and up

Summary: This is an excellent resource for high schoolers and adults. Known for their popular reference works, Dorling Kindersley has made a fascinating atlas that draws a person in to browse and learn. Contains over 450 detailed maps of every region in the world, including large fold-out maps, supported by interesting text and hundreds of photographs and diagrams.

The Kingfisher Geography Encyclopedia

Author: Clive Gifford
Publication: Boston: Kingfisher, 2003
ISBN: 0753455919
Description: 488 pages, ages 9–14

Summary: After an introductory section on the physical earth, this geography encyclopedia gives an overview of each country, organized by continent. Most nation entries are a page or less; some nations, like India, are given more space. Entries include text, photographs, maps, the national flag, and a sidebar of facts. This graphically appealing book is best for browsing; the information is not comprehensive or in-depth enough for most research and report needs.

How People Live

Authors: Penelope Arlon, Dena Freeman, Lorrie Mack, and Zahavit Shalev
Publication: New York: DK Publishing, 2003
ISBN: 0789498677
Description: 304 pages, ages 9–12

Summary: This beautiful book describes different parts of the world and how people live in each, from the Eskimos and Inuit of the Arctic to the Amish and Maya of North America and the Asante and Zulu of Africa. Organized in two-page spreads full of color photographs and short paragraphs, this is a good book for browsing and for bringing the world and its peoples to life, though not for extensive research since each topic is treated briefly. Each continent is introduced by a two-page overview that includes a political map, photographs, and quick facts. This is followed by a two-page overview of the people of the continent, and then two-page chapters on individual countries, regions, or people groups. Older students and adults would enjoy this book as well.

If the World Were a Village: A Book about the World's People

Author: David J. Smith
Illustrator: Shelagh Armstrong
Publication: Toronto: Kids Can Press, 2002
ISBN: 1550747797
Description: 32 pages, ages 9 and up

Summary: Helpful even for older students, this picture book imagines the whole world as a village of 100 people so that statistics are easier to grasp. In this global village of 100 people, 22 people speak a Chinese dialect, 20 earn less than a dollar a day, and 60 are always hungry. Each spread focuses on a different issue, such as religion, language, or literacy. At the end of the book, the author includes ideas for helping children develop an awareness of the world's people and geography.

Earth from Above for Young Readers

Photographs: Yann Arthus-Bertrand
Text: Robert Burleigh
Illustrations: David Giraudon
Publication: New York: Harry N. Abrams, 2002
ISBN: 0810934868
Description: 77 pages, ages 9 and up

Summary: This creative book presents thirty-four arresting aerial photographs of scenes from around the world, including fishermen in Morocco, a farm on the island of Crete, and a mangrove forest in New Caledonia. While not a reference tool, this book is great for browsing and piquing kids' interest. Locator maps show where in the world each photograph was taken. Informative text accompanies each photo.

Internet Sites

These are some of the excellent online sources for learning about the nations of the world.

https://www.cia.gov/cia/publications/factbook/index.html

This is the online version of *The World Factbook,* the U.S. government's geographical handbook featuring profiles, maps, and flags of all the nations. The site provides rankings of the world's nations for many features, including area, population, life expectancy, and gross domestic product.

http://cyberschoolbus.un.org/infonation3/menu/advanced.asp

On the United Nations Cyber Schoolbus—InfoNation site, students can view and compare statistical data for countries that are part of the United Nations. Data is available on population, economy, health, technology, and environment themes. Students can view profiles of individual nations or generate graphs to compare data for several nations at a time.

www.nationalgeographic.com

The National Geographic web site is fun to explore and has several useful subsections. The site for educators (www.nationalgeographic.com/education) includes lesson plans, mapping resources, geography games, and photographs from around the world. It has links to the National Geographic Bee (with its daily GeoBee Quiz), the National Geographic Student Atlas, MapMachine, National Geographic Explorer magazine, and more. The site for kids (www.nationalgeographic.com/kids) includes links to features from National Geographic's children's magazines and other fun activities. In the National Geographic online store, you can find many resources for sale, from maps to books like the *National Geographic Bee Official Study Guide* to games like the National Geographic GeoBee Challenge Game, a board game for learning about countries, landforms, cultures, history, and environment.

www.infoplease.com

This site has a wealth of information, including an online almanac and atlas and access to *The Columbia Encyclopedia.* You'll find world geographic information, country profiles, trivia, maps, and flags. Note that this site contains advertisements.

http://lcweb2.loc.gov/frd/cs

The Library of Congress Country Studies Series presents a description and analysis of the historical setting and the social, economic, political, and national security systems and institutions of countries throughout the world. This site is not designed for children, but it is a rich resource for the teacher's own research or for advanced students.

www.state.gov/r/pa/ei/bgn

The U.S. Department of State Background Notes include facts about the land, people, history, government, political conditions, economy, and foreign relations of independent states, some dependencies, and areas of special sovereignty. This is a good source for the teacher's own information gathering or for older students.

http://travel.state.gov/travel/cis_pa_tw/cis/cis_1765.html

U.S. Department of State Consular Information Sheets are available for every country of the world. Because their purpose is to help U.S. citizens make decisions concerning travel, they provide an interesting view of current conditions in a nation. The information sheets include such information as unusual immigration practices, health conditions, political disturbances, unusual currency and entry regulations, crime and security information, and drug penalties. This site is not designed for children, but older students might be interested in these up-to-date assessments of life on the ground in the nations they're studying.

www.usgs.gov

The U.S. Geological Survey, the nation's largest civilian mapping agency, provides educational resources for primary and secondary grades.

Subscription-Based Sites

You may have access to excellent subscription-based resources through your school or community library, either in the library or remotely from your own computer. Ask your school or library if they subscribe and whether you can access the sites remotely.

Lands and Peoples

The *Lands and Peoples* subscription site (http://lp.grolier.com) is the single most helpful resource we've discovered for learning about the countries of the world. Featuring articles, maps, photographs, and charts, *Lands and Peoples* is an excellent means for students to explore countries, cultures, and current events. The site is divided into five main sections. The *Encyclopedia* includes accessible feature articles on the world, the continents, the nations, and for North America, regions and states/provinces. Articles are accompanied by full-color photographs and maps and a listing of related web links. The *Global News Desk* provides weekly cultural interest articles focusing on different areas of the world, along with a weekly lesson plan for using the article with students. Using the *Culture Cross* feature, students can compare the land, people, economy, history, or facts and figures of any two continents, countries, or states/provinces. The *Electronic Atlas* is superb, with hundreds of maps, including special maps on climate, culture, economy, environment, exploration, geology, history, and population. The *Passport to Fun* section provides educational games and quizzes. Finally, the *L&P Almanac* includes charts and tables, a glossary of geographical terms, and other resources. A print version of *Lands and Peoples*, available in many libraries, contains the *Encyclopedia* portion of the site's resources.

CultureGrams Online Database

The CultureGrams Online Database (http://online.culturegrams.com/secure/index.php) is also an excellent resource for studying the countries of the world. This subscription site has two editions, one for kids and one for older students and adults. The country reports can be viewed online or downloaded as pdfs. The site also includes national recipes, information about famous citizens, excellent photographs that can be viewed as slideshows, downloadable map pdfs, and a seventy-seven-page pdf of teaching activities covering three grade groupings.

The Blackbirch Kid's Visual Reference of the World

This is a Thomson Gale e-book accessible online through many libraries. Each nation's entry can also be viewed or downloaded as an attractive pdf, which is more engaging and easier to read than the online format. The entries begin with facts at a glance and include text, locator and country maps, photographs, and several graphs highlighting such themes as religions, ethnic makeup, exports, and land and population ranks. Altogether, the book presents more than twenty-five hundred graphs, charts, maps, and photos covering all the countries of the world.

eLibrary: Maps

This subscription site (www.proquest.com) has maps from magazines, U.S. and foreign newspapers, radio and television news programs, and reference books. This site is not designed for children. It is more appropriate for the teacher's own research or for older students.

Other Resources

Map Skills for Children

Publication: Wynnewood, Penn.: Schlessinger Media, 2004
Description: 3 DVDs, 23 minutes each (also available as VHS), grades K–4

This highly recommended movie series includes three titles: *A History of Maps, Making and Reading Maps,* and *Maps and Globes.* Students explore the many types and uses of maps, the differences between maps and globes, and the history of cartography. With fun live-action from Washington, D.C., interviews with cartographers, and helpful graphics, the series emphasizes the everyday use of maps and instructs students in the skills of map reading and mapmaking. New terms and concepts are presented effectively. Helpful teacher's guides are available online.

Geography Songs Kit

Producers: Larry and Kathy Troxel
Publication: Newport Beach, Calif.: Audio Memory Inc., 1990, 2004
ISBN: 1883028132

The thirty-three songs on this CD help preschool and elementary-aged children memorize country names and a few key facts by geographic region. While production quality is better on some songs than others, the catchy tunes and cultural flair of the music entice children to sing along. Before they know it, kids will be able to name the republics of the former USSR or the countries of the Middle East. The sixty-nine page accompanying workbook contains all song lyrics, plus coloring maps, coloring pages of landmarks, and a few puzzles. The kit also includes a poster-size coloring map with song lyrics printed on it. Find out more at www.audiomemory.com.

The Global Puzzle

Created by A Broader View of Atlanta, Georgia, this award-winning, three-foot puzzle for ages eight and up contains pieces shaped like all the world's countries, U.S. states, and Canadian provinces. Capitals are included, and population and area facts about each country are printed on the "oceans." Several continent puzzles are also available. Find out more at www.abroaderview.com.